HEY BY GEORGE! II

On the Northwest side of Wita Lake

George W. Denn

PRESS

DEDICATION

This book is dedicated to each and every person mentioned inside its pages. I thank our great Triune God - Father God, Jesus Christ, and Holy Spirit - for bringing you all into my life, and for giving me this gift so that I could write about our experiences that we've shared and the friendships that we've forged, that will hopefully last for all eternity!

Ephesians 1:3-14 Life Application Study Bible NIV: *Praise be to the God and Father of our Lord Jesus Christ, who has blessed us in the heavenly realms with every spiritual blessing in Christ. For he chose us in him before the creation of the world to be holy and blameless in his sight. In love he predestined us to be adopted as his sons through Jesus Christ, in accordance with his pleasure and will - to the praise of his glorious grace, which he has freely given us in the One he loves. In him we have redemption through his blood, the forgiveness of sins, in accordance with the riches of God's grace that he lavished on us with all wisdom and understanding. And he made known to us the mystery of his will according to his good pleasure, which he purposed in Christ, to be put into effect when the times will have reached their fulfillment - to bring all things in heaven and on earth together under one head, even Christ. In him we were also chosen, having been predestined according to the plan of him who works out everything in conformity with the purpose of* *his will, in order that we who were the first to hope in Christ, might be for the praise of his glory. And you also were included in Christ when you heard the word of truth, the gospel of your salvation. Having believed, you were marked in him with a seal, the promised Holy Spirit, who is a deposit guaranteeing our inheritance until the redemption of those who are God's possession - to the praise of his glory.*

Forward

I thought it would be fun to ask some of the people that I wrote about in this book to share in the experience of writing a forward for it. But I will warn you right off, with tears in my eyes, if I could be just half the man that they have made me out to be, it truly would be a wonderful thing! These are just common everyday people, like the common man and woman the book was written for - people that go to work or school every day, but very seldom get any recognition for what they do; people just like my ancestors on the cover of this book who had a hand in shaping my life. They had a deep belief in God, and I am fortunate to have had the opportunity to work the same soil as they did, often side by side with my Grandpa, Uncle Lowell, and Dad. I would have to say that these three men had the biggest influence on my life, good or bad! But far too often as I was growing up, I could see, as I can now; that the common man gets very little recognition. It was into this atmosphere of the common person that God chose to send his only Son, Jesus Christ, to save all of humanity from our sin, if we so choose! My hat is off to the common person, for your life has far more importance than any one of us can possibly fathom! Without further a-do, here is what several of these common people that I was so fortunate to meet had to say, whether it was someplace I had been or just right here the past couple of years 'on the Northwest side of Wita Lake!'

—George Denn

"I had the privilege of meeting George Denn the summer of 2007 at Heartland SEP, a Christian summer camp. He was my assistant counselor. I have to admit I was intimidated by having someone twice my age being my assistant. My fears couldn't have been more baseless. George became a dependable and close friend, a wealth of knowledge and stability, not only for me, but for everyone else who came into contact with him.

George served as my rock during that week. He just had that down home wisdom that only years of being a farmer and relying on God can provide. George gave me a copy of his first book, <u>Hey By George!</u> while I was there; it was really refreshing to see that simple wisdom, and even more importantly to hear of God working so powerfully though his life.

I hope you enjoy reading this book and hearing the stories that George has to tell. I have no doubt that you'll get something out of it, and that God will use his stories to touch your life. God bless and enjoy."

—Michael Yegerlehner

"Ever so often a person needs a little help from a friend. I was that person and George was that friend. The form of help was taking my son to his farm. There George taught him not only farm chores but how to see things in a different view. This same young man who was heading to a life of darkness is now three years later starting college next semester.

As you read this book, see how George sees the world through 'God colored' glasses. Enjoy his real life stories, but more than that, let them enrich your life in Christ!"

—Denise Marie Olson

"George Denn is a 'complex' man who lives a Christian life. I've come to know George through family about three years ago. Ever since then, he has taught me the value of hard work and how to put things into a Christian prospective. George always seems to find the good in things, and people! Anyone who has had the opportunity of becoming acquainted with George over a cup of coffee knows that he has had a very fascinating life! One of those fascinating accomplishments he has done is write this book that you are about to read. This book is filled with inspiring scripture, as well as his stories. George has a great gift when it comes to writing, which he uses to glorify Christ. George has a little bit of helpful Christian advice for anyone in these wonderful stories. One can say that George changes and continues to change people's lives in a great way. I have had a very blessed opportunity to work with George. I will never meet another kinder hearted friend and employer like George again. I only hope George will continue to spread the gospel as Christ has attended him to. I hope this book will touch you in the same way as it has touched my life. Many blessings to you all!"

—Ethan Gibson

"George has always said that a person's life is a deep, deep thing. And the same is true of him. George is one of the few people that I can call a true friend, and a true friend is a rare thing. To watch George live his life is to truly watch Christ living His life through a person. Knowing George for over five years now, and having worked on his farm has made a huge impact on my life. God has used George and his stories to disciple and grow me in my walk with Christ. I know that as you read these stories He will do the same for you. Some things just can't be entirely understood, but one thing is for sure - that God is at work on the Northwest side of Wita Lake! To God be the glory!"

—Brad Claggett

"You don't have to look very hard to find God at work! Here is an opportunity to see God working through a man who's trying to live a simple life, but by no means is George a simple man. George has the ability to see God at work, and find his message of hope through every day events and through the people that come and go in George's life! It is my hope that you will be inspired by these stories and will see that God is with us always"

—Linda M. Gibson

"As I look back at all the things that George has talked about in his stories, and what he and I, as well as other friends of ours, have been through together on George's farm by Wita Lake, there have been many good times, as well bad times. But the important thing to look at in George's stories is how God truly works through these times of trial and error. God has used George's farm to create friend-ships that will last a lifetime. George's pumpkin business started out small, but has continued to grow like the friendships that have grown on George's farm. Ever since the summer of 2001 when I started working for George until now, I've gone out to his place to get away from everyday life and to be surrounded by God's natural beauty on Earth, and that's nature out in the country. It has always been an escape 'go-to place' for me to remember how awesome he and his creation are, and to take the time to see them. I believe George's farm place is a piece of heaven that God laid out for those like George, and everybody who wants to see God's true beauty. All and all, the experiences that George shares with you all in his books are not just stories; they are living proof of God's work and true beauty!"

—Troy A. Peterson

"Pumpkins. Squash. Corn shocks. George has told me a hundred times: "Thirteen years ago, if someone had told me I'd be growing pumpkins in the future, I'd have called them crazy and booted them off my farm!" Well, we all know that George grows pumpkins, and this fact is a blessing to us all.

I worked with George for a fall harvest season picking pump-kins, stocking the stands and doing other chores around his farm. I have since realized that it is not only George's customers who are able to enjoy the fruits of his labor, but also his hired help; guys like me who are young and are just getting started on this journey called 'life'. George has been a sound example of virtues that I hold in high esteem: simplicity, faith, and trust- story after story throughout George's recent years tell of an abundance of miracles and answered prayers in the name of the Lord, Jesus Christ. And most are exclaimed with a lot of these '!!!'! They are only appro-priate. But I don't think there's one person in this business who has been transformed more than the famed "Hay by George" himself. He has and continues to patiently endure his own pain and hardship, and through it all, has learned a bit about what it means to say "Not my will, but yours be done." It is with great pleasure that I was able to work with George, and his friendship is one that I treasure. Wishing only the best to George Denn and to all who read his words. A brother and a friend."

— Joseph Kruse

HEY BY GEORGE! December 31, 2006

Psalm 77: 5-14: I thought about the former days, the years of long ago; I remembered my songs in the night. My heart mused and my spirit inquired: "Will the Lord reject forever? Will he never show his favor again? Has his unfailing love vanished forever? Has his promise failed for all time? Has God forgotten to be merciful? Has he in his anger withheld his compassion? Then I thought, "To this I will appeal: the years of the right hand of the Most High." I will remember the deeds of the Lord: yes, I will remember your miracles of long ago. I will meditate on all your works and consider all your mighty deeds. Your ways, O God, are holy what god is so great as our God? You are the God who performs miracles; you display your power among the peoples.

As I sit here by my cozy wood fire this New Year's Eve afternoon, I have to laugh at how quickly things can change! Just this morning I was driving home in the rain, and thought, "It looks more like October than the end of December!" Now six hours later there are six inches of snow on the ground. So I guess it gives me a chance to tell some stories about how I have seen God working in my life since my last story.

Last July, while I was working on the grain harvest, somehow I must've done something to my left knee. I was taking a bath one night, and I noticed that my left knee cap was way bigger than my right one. "Oh, great!" I thought. With summer camp only about a week away (and sometimes that can be pretty demanding), I thought I'd just ask the doc at the camp to look at it, as long as I was there. You see, part of me is still from the "farmers' old school." You don't go to doctor unless you are just about dead, or perhaps you can't get the bleeding stopped after a few hours on your own, or something of that nature. It probably would show a sign of weakness or something. I'm sure this is just "a farmer thing!" One time, my Dad got his foot run over by a tractor and after three weeks of limping around, I mentioned that maybe he should go and see a doctor, because maybe something was broken. "No," he said "It will probably get better soon," and added that it was my fault in the first place because I had left the tractor in gear! What he failed to mention was that he shouldn't have been starting the tractor in the way that he did in the first place! I think that's why they have those warnings in the operator's manuals, because it could lead to severe injury! So you can see the kind of cloth I was cut from!

Once I was at camp, I asked the camp doctor if he would look at my knee, as I felt I had water on the knee. He said that he wouldn't, as I had not signed the proper forms. I just thought to myself, "OK, I guess I'll have to figure something else out." After camp was over, I was visiting with my cousins from Monee, IL. Nancy told me that her husband, Ron, had water on his knees all the time and that I'd have to go to a doctor and they would remove it with a BIG syringe! Somehow the image I had in my mind about that made me grimace just to think of it. So when I returned home, I told my friend, Jeff, that I believed he had the gift of healing, as he was interested in that sort of thing. 1 Corinthians 12: 9 mentions this gift as "a gift of the Holy Spirit." Also, James 5:14-16 states,

"Is any one of you sick? He should call the elders of the church to pray over him and anoint him with oil in the name of the Lord. And the prayer offered in faith will make the sick person well; the Lord will raise him up. If he has sinned, he will be forgiven. Therefore, confess your sins to one another and pray for each other so that you may be healed. The prayer of the righteous man is powerful and effective."

Now I know God doesn't always choose to heal this way. Sometimes he uses doctors. But the thought of the syringe thing made me feel like I wanted to try this way first! Anyhow, I have seen this sort of thing work in the past, and I don't figure God included these instructions in his word if it wasn't so. As Jeff prayed for my knee, I could feel the spot getting real hot on the inside. Jeff also said he could feel something going on in there, and almost immediately I felt relief. But the next day the water was still there. I had not been healed instantly. We kept praying for it off and on for about three weeks. One morning I woke up and the water was gone! So was the pain. My knee had been healed! No syringe, no doctor, no cost! All I can say is "Thank you, Jesus!"

The next time I saw God at work in a big way was around the end of August and into September. I had absolutely no one lined up to help me pick pumpkins this year. The fellows that had helped me in the past had all moved on in life. My friend, Jeff, had asked me on several occasions in August what I was going to do. I told him I was relying on God to provide me with some help, as I had been praying for some helpers this fall. And until he provided, I guess it was just me and thirty acres of pumpkins to pick (which by the way, would have been impossible, as last year I had twenty-five acres and three helpers, and it took almost till the end of October to pick!) I was standing on the promise in Ephesians 3:20, which states *"Now to him who is able to do immeasurably more than we ask or imagine, according to his power that is at work within us."* On one of the last days of August, Troy Peterson, a brother of Jeff's and one of the guys that worked for me in the past, showed up one day, and said that he had felt led to stop out here. I told Troy of my dilemma and asked him if he needed a job for the next couple months. He said that it was a funny thing, but he was in need of some work after school, since he was between jobs. I figured my situation had improved by 100% - now it was me and Troy with thirty acres of pumpkins to pick!

On September 16-17 we had the "3rd Annual Pumpkin Thing" here at my farm. This is where people can come and donate time picking pumpkins for a fundraiser for the popular Christian winter camp, "Snow Blast." It was just a day after everyone had gone, when the friendly weatherman had some unfriendly news for me. Hard frost was predicted for early Wednesday morning. Hard frost is about the worst news a pumpkin farmer can have. It was way too early for that, and I just didn't have enough help to get everything picked by then. Tired and exhausted, I said "Lord, if you want me to continue working here and raising these pumpkins, I need your help. And if you want me to quit, I want you to freeze everything tonight. Then I will be done with it all, and I will start looking for something else to do! I'm not even going to cover anything up tonight. If you won't protect it, well, to hell with it all then! In Jesus' name I pray. Amen!"

Just the day before I said this prayer, my neighbor, Dave Gibson, called me, and asked if I needed some help. His son, Dan, was looking for some work, so I told him to send him over. Dan asked me if I needed any more help, as he could probably get his cousin, Ethan, to come, too. So Ethan came on Tuesday and now he is my hired man. I called Jeff and my mentor, Doug, and we had some prayers for the frost situation. Nighttime came and I said, "Everything is in God's hands now. There is nothing I can do." The next morning when I woke up, the first thing I heard on the radio was that it was twenty-eight degrees in New Ulm, a town twenty-five miles west of me. It was thirty degrees in Mason City, Iowa, ninety minutes south of me, and thirty-four degrees in Mankato, where I live. I had my answer! God chose to help me out! Doug called me from Wisconsin Dells, a town about three and a half hours southeast of me, and asked if it had frozen. I told him "No." He said that was a miracle, as his car windows were thick with frost. I got up that morning relieved, since I finally had some direction from God.

But this was also the week that I had promised to take Blossom Johnson, an elderly lady from my previous church, down to Wisconsin Dells. There was a Christian festival going on there from Thursday until Sunday, and she was to be reunited with some family members for the weekend. There was no way I was going to let this 86-year-old lady down! I had it in my mind that if nothing else, I would drive her down on Thursday, come back home, then go back and get her on Sunday…unless of course, God would have another miracle for me! That miracle would be to find and purchase another pickup truck for the boys to use while I was gone, because my old Ford was hammered beyond being hammered, and unsafe for even me to drive down the road, let alone those guys! Another miracle would be supplying the funds to buy a pickup, as I had zero money available that day and maybe a little less! Also, this was going to be one of my first busy weekends for selling pumpkins. In other words, it wasn't a good weekend to be gone!

At about 8:00 a.m. on Wednesday, I reckoned, "If God wants me to keep working with these pumpkins, he probably wants me to have a decent pickup to haul them around in, too!" So I said another prayer, "God, if it is your will that I have a safe pickup for the boys to use while I am gone, help me to find one and make it possible to buy it. In Jesus' name I pray. Amen."

I opened a local paper and noticed a pickup that had been advertised for three weeks for $975. I called the party. "Yep, I still have it," the man said. I went to look at it and an hour later, I wrote out a check for it. He didn't know it, but I was praying that he wouldn't cash it till about Monday! He told me it's a funny thing, though. Although other people called about the pickup, no one ever showed up to look at it except me. And I'd been wondering why someone hadn't bought it right away!

Now all I had to do was get everything finished, then I could head for the Dells! By 1:30 a.m. on Thursday, I was out of here! I stayed at my Dad's house that night and at 9:00 a.m. I picked up Blossom and drove to Wisconsin Dells. I had to go shopping for some clothes there, because I didn't have time to pack. Thank God for Wal-Mart stores! It always seems things just turn out by the width of a gnat's eyelash! Once again, thank you, Jesus!

By the way, the check for the pickup was good. When he cashed it on Monday, it didn't bounce!

In November, my Dad's cousin, Donna, was here from Monee, IL for a few weeks visiting. I thought it would be neat while Donna was here to have a big Thanksgiving dinner at Dad's house for the relatives. My sisters picked November 12 for the day to have it. I didn't much like the day they had picked, as I thought it was too early. I preferred November 19, but thought I would be quiet about it to keep the peace. Everyone that came really seemed laid back and enjoyed themselves, as they didn't have any other place that they had to get to! I really felt the presence of the Holy Spirit that day.

Little did I know what was to take place on November 19, the day I'd wanted to have our dinner. It would've been a disaster, as you will see! I guess God knows what he is doing. My friend, Steve, called me on the 19th and wanted to treat me to supper for some work that I'd done for him earlier. It seemed like that was one of those days that nothing was going right. I'd tried calling my Dad several times, but couldn't reach him. I wanted to talk with him because we were going to take Donna back to Monee the next day. When I went to shave, I couldn't find my razor. This is the razor that I've had for 30 years, so I kind of liked the thing. I looked all over the place two or three times in spots where it would normally be. I remember opening my travel case up real wide several times, but all that was in there was a tube of toothpaste and tooth brush. The best I could figure was that it fell off the corner of the sink and into the trash can that I had emptied and burned about a half hour ago! I thought, "Guess I'll have to use one of those disposable kinds that I don't like much. Oh, well."

I had a great lunch with Steve and afterwards I was going to drive across the parking lot to Wal-Mart to see if I could find another razor like the one I'd lost. I noticed that Dad had tried to call me on my cell phone. So I returned the call, but Dad didn't answer the phone - Donna did. She said" George, I really have some bad news for you." I thought something must've happened to Dad, so I said, "Well, let me have the news!" She said, "Your cousin, Peter, killed himself yesterday. They just found out about it and everyone is meeting at your Uncle Lowell's. Your Dad and your sister are over there now."

At first it took my mind a while to process information like that! I just drove to Wal-Mart anyway, looking for a razor. Then I thought "What the heck am I doing here? My family needs me now, and I need to get out of here and get to my uncle's place. I'll find a razor some other time." My cousin, Peter, lived in Alaska. He was 57 and was about the last person in the world you'd have thought would take his own life. I was really saddened by the news. I have a picture in my mind that I will always remember Peter by. The last time I saw him was in June, just after he'd heard about one of the stories I'd written. Let's just say we didn't agree on the point I was trying to make! Before I left, Peter gave me one of those big grins, looked me straight in the eyes and said "You take care of yourself," and gave me a big hug. That's how I will always remember him!

On the way to my uncle's home, I called my friend, Jeff. We prayed for the Holy Spirit to be present. I didn't know what to expect as I walked into the house. I remember asking God for the words to say.

There seems to be a process with just about everything that goes on down here on Earth. The same is true of death and the acceptance of it for those who are left behind to grieve. We grieve because we have lost someone dear to us. My cousin, Peter, believed in Jesus Christ, although his view about the Lord probably was different than mine. I heard him once state that he did believe in Jesus Christ. From what John 3:16 tells us, it is the belief in Jesus Christ that gives us eternal life, and not anything we have or haven't done! When someone dies, I always like to think of all the people who were in that person's life and had passed on earlier. I imagine the reunion that's taking place in heaven with those people! It kinda makes a person a little jealous to still be here on Earth!

As I left the house that evening, I knew that the Holy Spirit was in the house, as you could feel the peace among the sadness. I stopped at Dad's house and told them that the trip to take Donna home was still on. It would be a while before Peter's funeral would be scheduled here, since they would first have a service for him in Alaska. I went home and started getting ready to leave in the morning. I opened my travel case and there was my razor that definitely hadn't been there earlier! It seemed that God was telling me "I can take things away and give them back again!" Hmm, where have I heard that concept before?

We took Donna home and celebrated Thanksgiving Day in the town of Bourbonnais, IL at a place called Coyote Canyon. There was my Dad, his cousin, Delma, Donna, Donna's daughter, Nancy, her son, Mike and myself. So we had a great time! This was my second time in Bourbonnais. Two days earlier, I was visiting friends, Stephen and Lilly Hill. (If you ever meet those guys, ask them what a "scullbuster" is!) Little did I know that it would be the last time I saw my cousin, Mike! We got word a week later that Mike had died in his sleep. The cause of death was unknown at the time. One thing that was sort of strange - both funerals (Peter's and Mike's) were on the same day! I prayed for peace and comfort for Mike's family and emailed my prayers to Nancy. Nancy told Donna that as they were making arrangements for Mike's funeral, she could feel somebody (possibly me) praying for them. When they got home, they read the e-mail! Mike, too, believed in Jesus. He told me as much!

A week ago today, I was asked to do a communion meditation at the New Life Christian Fellowship in St. Paul, MN. They rent from St. Matthew's Lutheran Church. For about six weeks, I knew I was to do this. I chose to talk about Matthew 2:1-12. This was the story of the Magi, or Wise Men, if you prefer. It was interesting to see how God just gave me what to talk about and how he arranged everything to coincide with the rest of the service that day! I have to admit sometimes I just like to challenge myself! I found that there was to be a collection that day. Luke 6:38 says,

"Give and it will be given to you. A good measure, pressed down, shaken together and running over, will be poured into your lap, for with the same measure you use, it will be measured to you."

Here is how I figure this all works! I had $10 in my billfold, and I had enough gas to get home. So I put the $10 into the collection plate as it went by. After services were over, I had to give Janet and Vernon fifty pounds of wheat that we had agreed on for $10. Before I left the church, they gave me a card that had the same scripture verse that I had used during communion, Matthew 2, on the envelope! How did they know what scripture I was going to use? On my way home, I got into a traffic jam on I-35W. It was interesting watching the people get impatient! Several cars pulled out and tried going around, but were stopped ahead by some police. Several cars pulled out and went back the direction that they came from. I don't know where they went, because there were cars backed up as far as I could see. One guy thought he was going to cross the median, but got hung up in the process! (By the way, if you're ever in a traffic jam, it is helpful to know that patience is part of the fruit of the Holy Spirit. It says so right here in Galatians 5:22. Just thought I would mention it.) I figured it was no use getting excited. While I was waiting, I thought I would open the card that Janet and Vernon gave me. To my surprise, inside the card was $40. Thank you, Janet and Vernon for the gift! So once again, I was returning home with more than I went with! I wonder what God is trying to tell me?

Well, as 2006 fades into 2007, I will leave you with a quote that a pastor from Argentina used. It is one that I've pondered a lot over the past year. "If you want to see what you have never seen before, then you must do what you have never done before!" God's peace and abundant blessings to you all in 2007!

Your brother in Christ,

George Denn

HEY BY GEORGE!   **May 25, 2007**

Psalm 40:1-2: *I waited patiently for the Lord; he turned to me and heard my cry. He lifted me out of the slimy pit, out of the mud and mire; he set my feet on a rock, and gave me a firm place to stand.*

Actually, I am still waiting to be lifted out of the mud and mire! Once again it is springtime in Minnesota, and that's just part of farm life in this great state! It seems like I've been waiting for spring all winter, but I know one day everything will be green again. It seems like I've been waiting for God to give me some sort of direction lately, but he seems to be telling me, "George, you just have to wait!" But I know one day everything will turn green again overnight, and the soil will be dry again to plant. Someday too, God will give me a definite direction.

Isaiah 30:18: *Yet the Lord longs to be gracious to you; he rises to show you compassion. For the Lord is a God of justice. Blessed are all who wait on him.*

I've heard the statement, "When it seems that nothing is happening, God is up to something!" But all I can guess is "What is God up to?" Every day it seems I wait for something. I wonder when the fields will be dry enough to plant. I have to wait! When will I sell all of my hay? I have to wait! I sent my first book manuscript to the publisher five weeks ago, but I still have to wait until sometime in June before it's finished, and I wonder where that will take me. Guess I will just have to wait! I wonder how my pumpkins will do this year. Will it be a good year or a poor year? I have to just wait and see. I haven't received all of my pumpkin seeds that I ordered in December. I am still waiting for them. It also seems like most of the people I've been talking to lately seem to be waiting for something to happen in their lives, too.

(Two months later...) I have to laugh - I wrote that part of the story two months ago in March. I ran out of thoughts, so I just put down my pen and paper and had to wait until today for the Lord to

give me the time and more to write about. Today a guy by the name of Carl bought a screen door for the back door of my house. The old one got ripped off by an 80 mile per hour east wind! I have never heard of a wind like that coming out of the East! I was waiting for God to provide me with a door or with some money so I could buy a door. Carl said that he didn't have enough time to put it on just then and asked if could wait until he had time to do it.

We received about an inch of rain yesterday, and I can't do much around here today. So it looks like God has provided an open door, so to speak, to finish this story! When I started writing this story, I was wondering when it would be dry enough to be out working in the fields. At the time of this writing, I have everything planted! My hay was all sold about a week ago, and I will be cutting new crop hay in a week. The pumpkins all got planted - 55 acres of them! I have even started to cultivate them.

But today I am sitting in the recliner outside my house, enjoying the day. The lake is clear as glass, and the geese are the only thing disturbing the water as they swim with their newborn goslings. The wheat in the field in front of the house is almost knee high, and the birds are singing happily on this nice sunny late spring day. It is one truly worth waiting for, as Psalm 118:24 says: "This is the day the Lord has made; let us rejoice and be glad in it." Two months ago, I was wondering when my book would be finished at the publishers. Well, it is almost complete and will be out sometime in June. But even the process for that took more than a year and it's been all of seven years since I started to write it!

I was on a fishing trip/prayer retreat last winter in early February on Pelican Lake in Orr, MN with Tom K., Jeff P., Gordy L. and Andrew B. I was wondering at that time how I was ever going to finance the publishing of my book, as I had given the funds away to some folks that were losing their home. I just felt it is no good for a family to lose their home, and that if I didn't help them out, then nothing that I had written in my book would've had much meaning! It was up there in an ice house that the idea came to me that I should honor my father somehow with my book, since it is because of him that I am here! Exodus 20:12 says to honor your father and mother so that you may live long in the land the Lord your God is giving you.

After I returned home from this time of prayer and fishing, the idea for the picture on my book cover materialized. After I had this idea, almost immediately the funds for my book also turned up. It all just came together like it was God's timing!

Psalm 30:14-15: *"But I trust in you, O Lord; I say 'You are my God. My times are in your hands."*

Also on our way home from this trip, Jeff and I stopped off to visit with some friends for the evening. Jeff was telling a story about a time when he had ran out of gas and how he was helped by a stranger. Jeff had gone to take a shower when my cell phone rang. A friend of mine, Mary, called and asked if I would pray for her situation. She was out of heating fuel and she didn't know what to do, as she still owed the supplier for the last fill. Immediately after I prayed for Mary and said amen, my friend said "I will buy Mary a tank of fuel"! I thought this was interesting, as the two had never met! It is also very interesting that the next time I talked to Mary, she said she called the fuel company to see what she owed them. They told her that she had a credit of $91.

Job 11: 7-9: *Can you fathom the mysteries of God? Can you probe the limits of the Almighty? They are higher than the heavens. What can you do? They are deeper than the depths of the grave. What can you know? Their measure is longer than the earth and wider than the sea.*

As I had mentioned in my last story on December 31, 2006, the Lord had provided me with a new hired man. Ethan is his name. So while we were waiting for spring, we were sawing fire wood from all the trees that had been taken down from a tornado that went through here two years ago. Also there was a tremendous amount of dead Elm trees; we sawed up fifty monster pickup loads of wood last winter, and we had a goal of 100 monster pick up loads for this spring. We achieved this on May 16th and we immediately stopped cutting - we had reached our goal! Now it is Ethan's job to split and stack all that wood when he isn't busy doing other things! All I can say is, "Have fun, Ethan!"

One thing that happened about midway through our wood cutting adventure was that I saw this great big Ash tree that was across the creek on Blase's farm. So we cut the thing into sections and drug it across the creek. This big tree was split in three places. I was cutting through one of the splits, when the busted off tree kicked out at me and hit my shoulder, and I went flying about six feet or so! When I was able to get up, I couldn't remember if the saw was still running or not. My arm just hurt like you know what! I was thankful, though, that it hadn't been any worse. When I saw Ethan, he told me that all he saw was me flying through the air! Once again I have to rely on God for healing, because I have no insurance and even less money.

As I write this, that happened about six weeks ago. I can use my arm, but have little strength in it. But it is healing slowly. I also wrecked more saw chains on that tree, because when we drug it across the creek, it got a lot of sand in the bark. Sand to saw chains is like cryptonite to Superman - it makes them useless quickly! When we finished with that tree, I told Ethan, "Let that be a lesson to us both. Just because something looks good doesn't necessarily mean it is!"

2 Corinthians 11:14-15: *And no wonder, for Satan himself masquerades as an angel of light. It is not surprising, then, if his servants masquerade as servants of righteousness. Their end will be what their actions deserve."*

A few weeks ago just before I planted pumpkins, I took my pumpkin planter out of the shed. I wanted to widen the rows, as I felt they were too narrow for pumpkins. Pumpkins need a lot of space to vine and grow and stretch. Also, they are easier to cultivate in a wider row. As I was widening the row settings, I thought I would remove some of the parts that had been needed for the purpose that it used to serve, as a corn planter, but not necessary for planting pumpkins. As I was doing this, I was thinking how God does that to us who have given our lives to him. As he widens our boarders of influence, he takes away things that are no longer needed, or are in the way for the purposes that he has for us today; even if sometimes these things can be painful. God sees things that we don't, and most of the time (but not always), when we look back at what God has taken or pruned from our lives after some time has passed, it hardly seems like we miss them. I always have to remind myself that this world is not my home!

John 15: 1-2: *I am the true vine, and my Father is the gardener. He cuts off every branch in me that bears no fruit, while every branch that does bear fruit he prunes so that it will be more fruitful.* **Also verses 18-19:** *If the world hates you, keep in mind that it hated me first. If you belonged to the world, it would love you as its own. As it is, you do not belong to the world, but I have chosen you out of the world. That is why the world hates you.*

Once again, I have my friend Jeff praying for my arm. One day he was telling me after he started praying for my arm, that often when he prays for healing for a person, God gives that person an insight for other areas of the person's life! That is interesting, because since Jeff has been praying for my arm, I have been thinking a lot about the scripture in 2 Chronicles 7:15,

"If my people, who are called by my name, will humble them-selves and pray and seek my face and turn from their wicked ways, then I will hear from heaven and will forgive their sin and will heal their land."

What is God trying to tell me? I don't know! I do know that the land was cursed from the time of Adam and Eve because of their sin.

Genesis 3: 17-18: *To Adam He said "Because you listened to your wife and ate from the tree about which I commanded you, 'You must not eat of it,' cursed is the ground because of you; though painful toil you will eat of it all the days of your*

life. It will produce thorns and thistles for you, and you will eat the plants of the field."

I also know that when Jesus went to the cross, it broke the curse that was on humans, but I am wondering if the curse was also broken on the land? And if it was, why are we acting like the curse is still on the land? I have been praying for wisdom in all of this. James 1:5 says, *"If any of you lacks wisdom he should ask God, who gives generously to all without finding fault, and it will be given to him."* Just the other day, four of us had communion here and blessed the land. Since that time, the very next day, in fact, I sold the remainder of my hay and was able to purchase some weed chemical. Also, bugs were attacking my pumpkins. Today God sent a perfect rain and I see no bugs. (They did come back shortly after, though, and I was provided with some bug chemical to kill them by a neighbor!) I continue to ask the Holy Spirit to breathe life into this worn out soil, as my finances won't allow me to purchase fertilizer this year, but I would if I could. I am starting to see that God has his hands on my finances to get me to look to him for the answers instead of ways that I am familiar with. What is God up to in all of this? Guess we will just have to wait!

Romans 1:17: *For in the gospel a righteousness from God is revealed, a righteousness that is by faith from the first to the last, just as it is written: "The righteous will live by faith."*

God's peace and abundant blessings to you all!

Your brother in Christ,

George Denn

HEY BY GEORGE!   August 15, 2007

Proverbs 16:28 *The laborer's appetite works for him; His hunger drives him on.*

This year I had the opportunity to take part in two summer camps that my church sponsors. Northern Lights is the name of the camp that was held at the Eagle Bluff Nature Center near Lanesboro, MN. This was the first year for the Minnesota camp, and the folks that were in charge of getting this camp off the ground at one time came pretty close to calling camp off! Now looking back, it would've been a great tragedy if camp had been called off. I am sure that Satan would've loved it! Romans 5:3 says,

"Not only so, but we also rejoice in our sufferings, because we know that suffering produces perseverance; persever- ance, character, and character, hope. And hope does not disappoint us, because God has poured out his love into our hearts by the Holy Spirit, whom he has given us."

I was counselor for Group 1 boys. Richard Siedslag was my assistant counselor. We had four boys in our dorm: Sam, David, Jonah and Evan. Now, if you've ever had a dorm full of boys to look after for a week, having only four seemed too good to be true! As the week went on, the staff all pretty much agreed that we had just the right size camp for our first time out! Forty-nine in all: 14 staff, 26 campers and 9 mini campers. Betty Johannsen had to leave us after just a few days to be with her mother in Texas, who was seriously ill. But before she left, she was able to teach those who took over her role in arts and crafts class. One of the first activities was river canoeing. One thing I liked was even if you weren't paddling, you were still always going somewhere! I told my crew "Whatever you do, follow the path of the instructor." There was one group of girls that went ahead of the instructor, and several times they got stuck in mud or rocks!

There was also archery class, but I couldn't participate in it, along with many of the other activities, because my arm had been clobbered by that tree last spring, and it was still bothering me if I used it too much. We also had bird watching and star gazing activities. It amazes me how much you learn that you never noticed before, if you just sit there and look and listen. It makes me wonder how much our fast paced society is really missing.

There was also a rock climbing wall. I didn't climb because of my arm, but I did get to belay. When you belay, you are in a harness that is hooked to a pin in the floor. It's your job to keep the rope snug for the climber. So you both have to rely on one another. The one lesson I learned on my station was that almost always the climber would get half way up the wall and then stop. Only those that were greatly encouraged seemed to go to the top. Those that had little or no encouragement could go no higher! Proverbs 18:21 says *"The tongue has the power of life and death, and those who love it will eat of its fruit."*

One night we had a bonfire, and of course, we had the ever popular s'mores. But when it came time to put the fire out, someone had tipped the garbage can over that held the water to extinguish the fire! The camper that did this thought that rain had filled the garbage can. So he dumped it out so that he could put his empty soda bottle in it. That just goes to show you that things aren't always what they seem! So Jeff, the assistant camp director, and I asked Vivian Malcomson if we could use her golf cart to haul some water to put out the fire. She said we could, but only if she could go with us! So Jeff drove, Vivian sat back and enjoyed the ride, and I stood on the back holding the light. We three had a blast! For some reason, there is nothing more fun than sneaking around camp in the middle of the night! By the way, the ages of this trio was 45 to 80 plus!

There was also a "high ropes" challenge course. I helped the people get off at the end of the zip line. Once again, encouragement was a key factor for some to make it to the finish! One morning during some free time, the boys found an object that they found amusing! At first I told them to throw it away. Then, for a gag, I told them to put it in Richard's hat, just to see what he would say! All he said was "I'd better not take this home!" You'll have to ask Richard what it was because I am not going to tell!

The theme from the Minnesota camp as well as the Illinois camp, was "Cross my Heart and Hope to Live"! In the first chapel message, we were taught that without Jesus Christ in our lives, our hearts are separated from God and tend toward evil and not good.

Jeremiah 17:7: *The heart is deceitful above all things and beyond cure. Who can understand it?* Also **Romans 8:7:** *The sinful mind is hostile to God. It does not submit to God's law, nor can it do so."*

In Chapel 2, they talked about how the God who created the universe wants to be in an eternal relationship with you. This chapel was called "Rescue 411- Straight to the Heart". Galatians 1:3-5 says,

"Grace and peace to you from God our Father and the Lord Jesus Christ, who gave himself for our sins to rescue us from this present evil age, according to the will of our God and Father, to whom be glory for ever and ever. Amen.

One of the questions that was asked was, "Will you receive his help, or will you turn away, looking for something or someone else?" It finished with the statement, "God is calling you to be in a covenant relationship, living in fruitful union with him." Chapel 3 gave us the message that when we ask Jesus Christ into our lives, a miracle happens. God gives us a new heart - a heart transplant.

2 Corinthians 5:17-21: *Therefore, if anyone is in Christ, he is a new creation; the old has gone, the new has come! All this is from God, who reconciled us to himself through Christ and gave us the ministry of reconciliation; that God was reconciling the world to himself in Christ, not counting men's sins against them. And he has committed to us the message of reconciliation. We are therefore Christ's ambassadors, as though God were making his appeal through us. We implore you on Christ's behalf; be reconciled to God.*

God made him who had no sin to be sin for us, so that in him we might become the righteousness of God.

Chapel 4 was titled "The Heart of a Champion!" The opening question was "What was Jesus' heart like?" Jesus' heart is to die for us…so he could live for us.

John 17:1: *Father, the time has come. Glorify your Son, that your Son may glorify you.*

Jesus' heart is to share truth with us.

John 17:7-8: *Now they know that everything you have given me comes from you. For I gave them the words you gave me and they accepted them. They knew with certainty that I came from you, and they believed that you sent me.*

Jesus heart is to pray for us.

John 17:9: *I pray for them. I am not praying for the world, but for those you have given me, for they are yours.*

Jesus' heart is to protect us.

John 17:11 and 15: *I will remain in the world no longer, but they are still in the world, and I am coming to you. Holy Father, protect them by the power of your name - the name you gave me - so that they may be one as we are one. My prayer is not that you take them out of the world but that you protect them from the evil one.*

Jesus' heart is to set us apart.

John 17:17-19: *Sanctify them by your truth; your word is truth. As you sent me into the world, I have sent them into the world. For them I sanctify myself, that they too may be truly sanctified.*

Jesus' heart is the Heart of a Champion!

Chapel 5 was "Heart to Heart". God says to guard your heart. Proverbs 4:23 says *"Above all else, guard your heart, for it is the wellspring of life."* The last statement made was, "When the heart of Jesus is pumping his life's blood through you, his way of living will come out from you." One thing I want to mention that I never knew before is that the human heart pumps 8000 gallons of blood each day!

I guess I will have to say goodbye to the Minnesota camp for this year, even though I could write a lot more about it!

I came home from camp with just ten days to get my work done before I had to leave for Heartland camp in Illinois, but Ethan is around here now. At least he is supposed to be! So it's not quite as bad as it used to be. The first thing the Holy Spirit impressed upon me was to get the wheat bundles into the shed, as too much rain will ruin them as decorations. I had about a thousand of them to pick up. I got them picked up that first day home and we got over a half inch of rain that night! Later on that week, we got two inches. I think it's funny that we didn't get any rain all summer until now when I really need to get my work done!

The last day came and I had absolutely no money to go on, so my landlady, Doris, financed my trip. Some money came in very late that evening, so I was able to repay Doris before I left! I left home here at 8:00 PM on August 1. I had to get some new clothes yet because I had none with me, just my empty suitcase. Matt and Linda Gibson, Ethan's Mom and Dad stopped me at the end of my driveway. They asked if I'd heard the news that the I-35W bridge in Minneapolis had collapsed. I thought of all the times I had gone across that bridge the past few months, and wondered if I knew anyone that was on it when it went down. It turns out that I didn't. Anyway, I was finally able to buy a few clothes. I put them in my suitcase and said "I am packed!" I bought the rest of what I needed when I got to Illinois. It seems like I never get packed until I get to where I'm going! It kind of makes me feel like I've escaped from something!

The first thing that happened when I got to Eagle Crest Camp was a young lady by the name of Sharon had locked her keys in her car! David Holmes found us a coat hanger. I made a hook on the end, put it through the rubber edging of the door, hooked the plastic door lock and unlocked her door. This device reminded me of the ones I used to make for catching chickens once upon a time! After listening to some basic staff rules we had to go work in our assigned areas. Since I was a co-counselor and worked on security, I had to hunt up a log for Liz and Sarah for their team building challenge course. Then they had some of us staff go through the log course and I sure wished I'd found a fatter log!

In the evenings, there was always the friendly card game going on in the dining hall. Usually it was Bernie Bryant, Dave Salander, Dave Worsfold, and whoever else that happened by! They all seemed amused at how I play cards, but what I think is funny is how often I would win! One night a message came over the radio, "George, you are needed in the lunch room!" So I went there and got into a game of cards that lasted till 2:00 a.m. I am getting too old for those late nights!

I seemed to be unusually tired through the course of the camp, and if I sat around too long, I would doze off to sleep! The people that were involved with photography somehow would catch me each day in one of these sleepy moments, and the next day it would be posted on the previous day's slide show of camp events. Everybody seemed to get a chuckle out of that. I just told people I was in a moment of meditation! I really had to watch it, though, the day Tracy Porter was speaking, because last year at Wisconsin Dells, he was giving a message at the Fall Festival. I had fallen asleep when Tracy started shouting during his sermon. That suddenly woke me up and I kicked the lady in front of me and she got up and moved. Her husband told me that I was kicking her! At camp, Tracy was speaking about some guy named Munch who summed up that life on this Earth was a scream! That's funny, because some days I feel the same way! But I don't think Munch knew the Lord Jesus Christ and that helps a lot!

There were also hornets at camp this year. One hornets' nest was in a tree down by the girls' dorm. One way we knew that they were there was because someone had set up some orange marker cones that said "Beware of hornets!" Another way we knew that they were there was because people were getting stung! Also, out by the archery course, there was a big sack of them. We decided it was necessary to eliminate them because they were starting to disrupt camp. So on Monday night, Tracy, Stephan, Chris, Dave and myself set out on Operation Eliminate Hornet! While Dave was buying ice cream, Stephan and I quickly pulled a two layer garbage bag over the hornet nest down by the girls' dorm. Chris was holding the light and Tracy cut the branch. The first hornets' nest had been eliminated. We could hear them buzzing angrily inside the bag. We put the bag of hornets in the freezer. I thought it would be interesting to see the inside of it and show whoever might want to see it also. This all made Amy, our head cook, a little nervous, but later she was glad that she let me do that! The next morning I cut the hornet nest open. The sack was seven layers of paper towel-like material. From the top were three upside down "mushrooms", all connected to one another in the center. It made me wonder if hornets operate on some sort of caste system, where the more importance you have, the higher up in the nest you get to stay. The combs were full of larva, ready to hatch, so it was a good thing that we eliminated them! The next sack of hornets was too high in a tree to bag from the ground. We would've had to use a ladder. Also, there were many hornets on the outside of the nest, so we decided to spray them. Just like an Old West gun fight, we rode up to the place where the hornets were in our trusty golf carts. By this time, two guys from the Salvation Army camp wanted to get into the action. So armed with seven cans of hornet spray, we seven guys at the count of "One, two, three..." blasted those ornery critters to kingdom come! They didn't stand a chance, and that pretty much was the end of the "night of the hornet" and our hornet troubles!

Since our chapel messages were the same as the Minnesota camp, I won't repeat them. One of the activities that the boys were involved in was a special event based on the scripture from Ephesians 6:10-18:

Finally, be strong in the Lord and his mighty power. Put on the full armor of God so that you can take your stand against the devil's schemes. For our struggle is not against, flesh and blood, but against the rulers, against the authorities, against the powers of this dark world and against the spiritual forces of evil in the heavenly realms. Therefore put on the full armor of God, so that when the day of evil comes, you may be able to stand your ground, and after you have done everything, to stand. Stand firm then, with the belt of truth buckled around your waist, with the breastplate of righteousness in place, and with your feet fitted with the readiness that comes from the gospel of peace. In addition to all this, take up the shield of faith, with which you can extinguish all the flaming arrows of the evil one. Take up the helmet of salvation and the sword of the spirit, which is the word of God. And pray in the Spirit on all occasions with all kinds of prayers and requests, with this in mind, be alert and always keep on praying for all the saints.

In this activity, the boys started down below the steep hill at the camp. In the valley, we talked about how life is a series of hills and valleys. A few personal examples were shared and then we were ready to climb the hill. After we climbed the hill, we could have a drink of water before we were ushered to our stations. At each station, we were told how important that particular piece of armor was. Then a trumpet sounded and we would yell "Strength and Honor", and go to our next station. Time after time, I would be reminded of different people in my life who didn't think having the full armor on was all that important. I also recalled what happened to those individuals! It all reinforced in my mind how important it is to have on the *full* armor of God! If you are one of those people that think some of the armor of God isn't important, I wish you luck, because you will need it!

Another part of camp that touched me was during the awards ceremony when the young man that had stayed at my place two years ago received an award for being best camper in his dorm. As he went up to receive his award, I started to cry. If you could've seen the condition of this young man several years ago, and where he is today at age 17, you'd be amazed! I just think that is a testimony of what these Christian camps and the Holy Spirit working through us all can do! Another touching moment of camp was at the talent night when a young lady got up to sing, and the words just wouldn't come. Almost immediately, Karen got up on stage with her and comforted and encouraged her and helped her finish her song. The young lady received a standing ovation!

What would camp be without the dorms where the campers stay and are a part of? Let me introduce my dorm to you! Michael Yegerlehner was our dorm counselor. It was his first year as counselor and he did a great job! Jon and Carla Reinagel were our dorm parents or "Mom and Dad", as we called them. Joshua Zuniga was our dorm's big brother. Our campers were Quentin, David, Marcos, Aaron, Tim, Nate, Jordan, Tyler, Chris and Isaiah. I was the co-counselor for Dorm 3B (or 3M as we later called it - "all that is man!") One of the exercises we did as a dorm was to write our first name on the top of a piece of paper and hand it to the person to the left. They would write something about you, then they would hand it to the person to their left, until it eventually returned to you. I thought it would be fun to show what they wrote about me -unedited!

GEORGE

"George is a great writer, and he is very funny. Dear George, I have to tell you to keep up the good sleepy, sleepy head." - Nathaniel

"George, thanks for all the help and being the Rock in my dorm. I couldn't have done it without Christ working through you. Thank you for not judging me." - Anonymous

"It was cool to see you interacting with the kids - you bring so much peace into every situation, and you were a great help." - Jon and Carla

"He wrote his own book, which amazed me." - Chris

"I can't wait to read your book, I will love it I bet. You are so cool!" - Anonymous

"I have only read on your book 2 pages and it is so perfect. You add so much feeling. Hope you put us in your next book." – Marcos

"He shaved in the sink." - Anonymous

"George, I am so glad I met you this summer. You are an inspiration and my brother in Christ." - Anonymous

Awesome book writer, my most awesome friend and a wonderful person and loves God so much." - Ty

"George has strong faith in the Lord and is a very book publisher!" - Anonymous

I have to say that this camp touched me more deeply than any other I have been involved with! Now I am back in Minnesota on my farm cutting my final hay crop for the season. As I drive my tractor and mower back and forth across the field and see the cut hay being placed into a windrow to dry, I realize the most important work I did this past year was being at those two camps. I think I have come to a greater understanding of what Jesus meant in Matthew 6:19:

"Do not store up for yourselves treasures on earth, where moth and rust destroy, and where thieves break in and steal. But store up for yourselves treasures in heaven where moth and rust do not destroy, and where thieves do not break in and steal. For where your treasure is, there your heart will also be."

God's peace and abundant blessings to you all!

Your brother in Christ,

George Denn

HEY BY GEORGE!   November 29, 2007

Philippians 4:19: *And my God will meet all your needs according to his glorious riches in Christ Jesus.*

Now that the fall work around here is pretty much coming to an end, I find that I have time to write again. Being it is the Thanksgiving season, and the beginning of the Christmas season, it is time for me to reflect on the past year's happenings; and what a year it was! I want to concentrate, though, on the times when I have seen God's provision.

In the springtime, once again my finances were at an all-time low! Poor Ethan, my hired man, a couple of times there was quite a space between the times that I could pay him! I like to borrow a statement from an old movie that I like to watch: "If sugar was two cents a barrel, I couldn't have bought a pinch of salt and an egg to fry it on!" Now that's low! But I have finally realized that God has been allowing that condition in my life so that I keep looking to him for the answers, instead of leaning on my own understanding! Proverbs 3: 5-6 says, *"Trust in the Lord with all your heart and lean not on your own understanding; in all of your ways acknowledge him and he will make your paths straight."*

One day last spring, I had a six acre field to work up for planting gourds. When I climbed into the tractor, the fuel gauge registered just a little bit above empty. I thought "God will supply my need", and since faith always requires action, I headed to the field, worked up the piece of ground, and returned to the yard, and parked my tractor. The next morning my neighbor, David, called me, asking if I had enough fuel to do the rest of my spring field work. I told him I was out and he suggested that I should come over and get some from him so I could finish up. I went and got about 90 gallons of fuel and put it in my tractor. I started it up and as usual, it started immediately; but just as quickly, it shut off again. I had used up every bit of fuel the day before! Once again Jesus showed me that I had plenty for the day at hand, both for yesterday and for today! (Even though I wasn't exactly comfortable with what he had given me.) Sometimes

I still have to be reminded what is a want and what is a need. Most of the time I find they are vastly different.

Another time I saw God at work in my finances (or probably more accurately, came to my rescue) was at spring planting time. I needed some red clover seed so I went to Gene Werner Seed Farm. Gene is a guy I have bought seed from for years. The bill for the clover seed came to $1540. I asked Gene if he would hold a check for me until May 15th. Gene started to laugh, "For one year or two?" he asked me? Laughing in return, I told Gene "Better make it three; maybe by then my ship might come in!" I had to call Gene to hold the check a few days longer, as I had arranged to haul some oats to sell. The only problem with these oats was that they had already been bought and paid for by some other party. I was only holding them! In farmer terminology this process is merely called "borrowing from Peter to pay Paul"! You will have to bear with me for a while to see how this all turns out, because technically, I just stole the oats and as a Christian, I know that stealing is a sin. So I had to ask God for forgiveness for my sin of stealing the oats!

1 John 1:8-10: *If we claim to be without sin we deceive ourselves, and the truth is not in us. If we confess our sins, he is faithful and just, and forgives us from all unrighteousness. If we claimed we have not sinned we make him out to be a liar, and his word has no place in our lives.*

Well, my friend Chris hauled the oats, but he arrived way too early in the morning to bring back a check. So they told him that they would send him the check, and Chris would call me as soon as the check came. Finally on Monday evening I got the check. The oats were hauled on Thursday so that was a five day wait! It seemed that no matter how hard I tried to make Gene's check good, I couldn't. It bounced before I could get the money to the bank and I was charged the usual $25 overdraft fee! I decided to wait until Gene called about the check. I had some cash for him now instead of a check, and I needed to return a few bags of seed, anyway. One week went by - no call. Two weeks went by - no call, and no sign that the check was sent back through the bank. I started to wonder if

God had made the check disappear. I had that happen once before, you know! Since I was strapped for cash, I slowly started using the money for other expenses around the farm, but never for anything that wasn't a need! I just shook my head some days thinking "Oh, what a tangled web we weave!"

Oats harvest had just begun when I returned home from Summer Camp Number 1. They had just taken one truckload out of the field. I went in the house to check my phone messages. Dan down at Equity Supply left me a message that they needed some oats ASAP. I called Dan first thing Monday morning, telling him I had a load of oats for him, and that we would bring it right down. Boy, was that a close shave! The load of stolen oats had been returned! Thank you, Jesus!

I was still wondering whatever happened to the check I had given Gene. Sometime in late September, I got a call from Gene. He said, "George, I have been sitting on this check since last spring and was just wondering if you wanted to make good on that." I told Gene I could give him $1200 in cash, but I needed some winter wheat seed. So I was just wondering if he would allow me to include the balance of $340 in with the check for the winter wheat seed, and if he could hold that check until Monday! Gene said "Sure, I can do that." When I went to pick up the seed, I asked Gene why it had taken him so long to call me about the check. He said that when he got the check back from the bank, he put it in a drawer meaning to call me. But some other stuff got piled on top of it and he forgot about it until his wife was cleaning out the drawer, found it and told Gene that he should call me! So all's well that ends well, I guess!

I also found out that Mrs. Werner, Gene's wife, used to teach V.B.S (Vacation Bible School) with my great aunt, who was a Catholic nun, Sister Ethel Denn. I find all of this very interesting!

The second time I had to use one of my "walking on the water checks" I was planning on going to a pastors meeting in Ramsey, MN on the last weekend of June. But my Dodge pickup was in the shop and I needed $901 to pay the repair bill! I told Doug Johannsen about this earlier in the week, and asked that he would be praying about that for me. Friday came and my situation hadn't changed any. It constantly amazes me that I always have to take a step and do something, and then I have to wait to see what happens and how God works it all out! Now you see, I absolutely was not going to miss this meeting. I needed the fellowship in the worst way, and most of these folks I only get to see once or twice a year. Also, a church service and a potluck picnic were scheduled the next day, and as most of you know, a single man won't pass up a free lunch no matter how dire the circumstances! So I wrote Lagers Chrysler a check for $901. Doug called me to see if my situation had improved, and I had to tell him what I did! I also mentioned that I was "walking on the water", so to speak with my checkbook! He asked me if I had ever heard the phrase "There is no fool like an old fool!" "Yeah," I told him, "but I thought that only pertained to an old man chasing a young woman!" Doug's wife, Betty, gets really nervous when she hears my name and writing checks in the same sentence! She figures that just about anything can happen and most times it usually does!

As it turned out, I went to the meeting and a friend of mine gave me a check for $250! I asked him, "What is this for?" My friend said, "I want you to come and see me sometime. That's money for gas." So I told him I would be up next weekend. I went to the church service the next day. We held it at a picnic area at Lake Johanna in the town of Arden Hills. During the church service when the offering was taken, I decided to put in all I had, nine dollars, just to see if God had anything interesting to show me that day. Later on after lunch, several of us were playing cards. The game was called "Stab Your Neighbor". That sounds like a card game that Christians should be playing, now doesn't it! It was Bill Mason's game and deck of cards, so you'll have to talk to him about that. During the game, Betty Johannsen came up to me and said, "George, I found this laying on my hat." It was the check for $250 that my friend had given me. I hadn't even noticed it was missing! God showed me then and there that he could do anything he wanted with these pieces of paper we call checks!

Once again, one week later the check I had written for $901 bounced and I was charged the $25 overdraft fee. The check didn't come through the bank again until the first week in August. More than a month had gone by. The only problem was that I was leaving for Summer Camp Number Two in Illinois at the same time that I found out the check had bounced again! All I could do was put a check that I had received into the night depository at the bank in case it came through the bank again while I was gone. Finally one day in September, I received a call from Lagers Chrysler. The message on my phone said, "Mr. Denn, we have a returned check here from you and we were just wondering if you can take care of this." On Monday morning I walked into Lagers, and told them who I was, and that I understood that they had a returned check. "Oh, yes," they said, "for $901." I told them that I was sorry for any inconvenience that it had caused. They told me that it was quite all right, that that sort of thing happens and that they were just glad I had come in and taken care of it.Once again, all I can say is "Thank you, Jesus!"

In July the brakes went out on my old Ford pickup that the Lord had provided the fall before. Ethan, my hired guy, accidentally backed into a loaded hay wagon and smashed the back end. My thoughts at that time were like that of Job in Chapter 1:21: *The Lord gave, and the Lord has taken away. May the name of the Lord be praised.* I knew where there was another pickup for sale. I first noticed it last fall when I delivered hay to its owner, Rock King. I remember thinking, "It would sure be nice to have that pickup, but I really need to be satisfied with what God has given me." I stopped in at Rock's place and mentioned that I noticed that he had a pickup for sale, and I was wondering if he might want to trade some hay for it, as I was a might short on cash at the time. No, he said, he was selling some of his livestock and he wouldn't be needing as much hay as he had in the past. I asked him if he would hold a check for awhile. Yes, he could do that, he said. So I wrote out a check to Rock for $3000, dated October 6, three months away! I told Rock that if I could make it good any sooner, I would call him. We shook hands, signed the title, and I was back in business! I made sure that when October 6 rolled around that I had the money in the bank! On the 10th of October I received a call from Rock King's daughter saying that they looked all over for the check that I had given them for the pickup. Somehow the check had vanished, and they were wondering if I would issue them another check. "Certainly," I said. I told them that I would stop over, since I drive by their place every day. When I gave the check to Rock, he told me that not only was the check missing, but also the file that it was in, as well! I remember telling God as I drove away, "Man, are you good! God, not only did you make the check disappear, but even the entire file that it was in!"

In early summer I was watching the weeds start to take over some oats. I was thinking of how Jesus cursed the fig tree in Matthew 21:18-22.

Early in the morning, as he was on his way back to the city, he was hungry. Seeing a fig tree by the road, he went up to it but found nothing on it except leaves. Then he said to it, "May you never bear fruit again!" Immediately the fig tree withered. When the disciples saw this they were amazed. "How did the fig tree wither so quickly?" they asked. Jesus replied, "I tell you the truth, if you have faith and do not doubt, not only can you do what was done to the fig tree, but, also you can say to this mountain, 'Go throw yourself into the sea,' and it will be done. If you believe, you will receive whatever you ask for in prayer."

I remember telling the Lord one day, "Lord, I guess I don't have the faith it takes. The weeds just won't die when I ask them to!" I also remember selling some hay almost immediately, and how Howard Guse called his chemical rep. and ordered the weed chemical that I needed, as we were delivering the hay! So I was able to spray the weeds the next day and the weeds did die - just not the way I thought they should. So I guess I do have that kind of faith after all!

About the same time the bugs were eating up my young pumpkin plants. My neighbor, David, called just at that time to see what I was up to. I told him I was cultivating pumpkins, but I didn't know why, because the bugs were eating them up! "Why don't you spray them?" he asked. "Because I didn't have the money to spray them," I said. He told me to call the co-op and charge some bug spray to his account. "I won't do that," I said, "but if you got the spray, I would accept it!" Two hours later Jeff, a guy from the co-op, dropped off the spray. God did answer my prayers using modern means!

As summer turned into fall, Ethan and I got ready for the pumpkin season, but in the back of my mind I also knew that Ethan and I weren't going to be able to pick 55 acres of pumpkins all by ourselves! What would Jesus have us do?

Matthew 9:37: *Then he said to his disciples, "The harvest is plentiful but the workers are few. Ask the Lord of the harvest, therefore, to send out workers into his harvest field."*

Here's what happened when I did that. One day before we started to pick, Ethan told me that his mom, Linda, and sister, Kelsey, wanted to help pick pumpkins to earn some extra money. "Okay," I told Ethan, "you can be their boss." Later, Linda asked Katy Schultz if she wanted to help her pick after Kelsey found out that picking pumpkins wasn't her cup tea! For the longest time, I would call Katy by the wrong name. I forget now what I called her; also, she was a very good sport when I showed her my "gourd trees"! The vines grew up the trees and gourds were hanging from the branches. It took her a while to figure it out that I was pulling her leg, but we all had a good laugh anyway! Katy could pick pumpkins as well as the guys so I was glad she came to help! Linda also rounded up Steven and Dylan Herme. They are twins. Steven hardly ever said anything, and Dylan never stopped talking! I enjoyed working with and getting to know them both and felt blessed that God had sent them. Ethan also convinced his friend, Mike Clobes, to come. His nickname is Boomba. Mike was like the Paul Bunyan of the group. I could tell that he has a heart as big as he is, even if he likes to tease everybody. (I have the very same frailty myself!) God bless you, Mike, a thousand times over!

One day my neighbor, Mary, stopped to talk as Ethan and I were unloading some pumpkins. She told me that her nephew might be looking for some work. I told Mary just to send him over, so one day Joe Kruse came to talk to me, and I told him he had a job. Joe is the kind of person who likes everybody, and everyone likes him. Joe turned into one of my main workers and stayed till the work was totally done in the fall! Joe is also a drummer and is planning a trip to Europe in the spring. I feel God has big plans for Joe's life! I sure am going to miss Joe when he leaves, as I feel I have found a new friend.

Towards the end of pumpkin picking, Brad Claggett flew up from Oklahoma to help us finish the season and to help split all the wood that Ethan and I never got around to doing. Brad and his new bride, Kelly, were here a month earlier on their honeymoon. During their stay they even cleaned my house! Now, if that wasn't from God, I don't know what is!

The fall wasn't the best as far as the weather was concerned. This year once again we had an early frost scare, even earlier than last year. Dylan, Joe and I prayed one night for God to protect the squash, as we had done our best to get them picked, but our best wasn't enough. Once again God protected them for us! It rained most of October. Some days we were up to our knees in mud, and we even had to pick some out of standing water! My friends, Terry and Robert, also helped pick when they could. We had four fundraisers for the Lutheran school that Linda arranged. Also, we had the yearly fundraiser called "The Pumpkin Thing" for my church's winter youth camp, "Snowblast". I know that God sent every single person this fall to help out! For practically 61 days, through rain and mud, heat and cold, we never stopped picking pumpkins except for one day! I feel truly blessed to have met every person who helped me this fall, for I feel they are the important ones! They are the ones that took my ideas and turned them into reality, and made this fall, once again, the best one ever! I pray that God blesses each one in a mighty way! Just as quickly as each one showed up, one by one they left here and went back to the other things in life that God had for them to do.

Before Thanksgiving, Joe and I took Brad back to Oklahoma. Now Joe and Ethan are busy stacking the last of the wood. Just a few more days and the work will be done for another year. Ethan is going to work for his uncle next year. I will miss him. He was a good worker - one of the best I've ever had! Joe is planning his trip to Europe in the spring, God willing. In some ways, this is a hard time of year for me, because as everyone leaves, they seem to take a part of me with them. I guess I just get too attached to people! There is one thing that always seems to remain constant around here, though, and that's the scene that I've taken in every fall that seems so peaceful to me. As I walk up the old dirt road that's behind my house, overlooking the plowed fields, resting until springtime, I see the soft glow of light coming from the living room windows of my old farm house. I just know God will take care of me in the future, just as he has these past 45 years!

Philippians 4: 20: To *our God and Father be glory for ever and ever. Amen.*

God's peace and abundant blessings to you all!

Your brother in Christ,

George Denn

HEY BY GEORGE!   **December 16, 2007**

Luke 2:8-14: *And there were shepherds out in the fields nearby, keeping watch over their flocks at night. An angel of the Lord appeared to them, and the glory of the Lord shown around them, and they were terrified. But the angel said to them, "Do not be afraid. I bring you good news of great joy that will be for all the people. Today in the town of David a savior has been born to you; he is Christ the Lord. This will be a sign to you: You will find a baby wrapped in clothes and lying in a manger." Suddenly a great company of the heavenly host appeared with the angel and saying "Glory to God in the highest and on earth peace to men on whom his favor rests.*

As I was writing down the above scripture, I was thinking back to my boyhood days and how there always seemed to be some sort of rivalry between those of us who were of "country origin" and those who were from town. Now that I have a few years under my belt, I can plainly see that God loves those from the city just as much as those from the country! Also it seems nowadays some of the country people I know view their city brethren as better off – materially, that is. I don't agree, for I do not believe that's what true wealth is!

I thought it would be fun to share with you some stories that I have never written about until now. I have told these stories to a few people over the years, and now, being the Christmas season, the time of sharing, I thought I would share them with you. Since I was born, raised and spent my entire life right here on this farm (so far anyway), my city brethren will have to bear with me, as these tales definitely come from a country point of view!

My first story took place around Christmas sometime in the mid-1960's. As I recall, Christmas wasn't the commercialized holiday that it has become today, at least not in our family. I know my Mom would never decorate anything until around the 20th of December, no matter how hard we begged her! I always remember us having a Christmas tree. Mom would put candy canes on the tree as the finishing touch of her decorating. I remember sneaking these candy canes off the tree when she wasn't looking, and the many times she told me that Santa Clause wouldn't come if I was naughty didn't stop me at all! In fact, it probably enhanced my desire for them! They were just way too tempting for me. As a matter of fact, I am eating one as I am writing this! Mom had the best hearing of anyone I've ever known. So I found out that the best times to sneak a candy cane from the tree were: Number 1: When she went outside to take care of her chickens; Number 2: When Mom went into the basement to wash clothes. (Wringer washers of that day were noisy and required a lot of time to run!) The Number 3 best time to sneak a candy cane was when Mom went upstairs, but I had to be quick, as it was often very cold up there, and she didn't seem to stay up there very long! But try as I may, she always seemed to know when one candy cane was missing and where it disappeared, too!

This particular tree that we had one year for some reason didn't look like the others we've had in the past. There was something different about it, but my young mind couldn't figure it out. On one of my candy cane sneaks, I noticed twine string in several places inside the tree wrapped around and tied. It didn't make sense to me, as I had only seen this stuff on the hay bales that were down in the barn. Or they were hanging from a nail in the barn because that's where Dad put them when he broke the bales to feed the cows their hay. So when I saw the twine on the tree, it seemed out of place to me. At about the same time, I also noticed some branches had been sawed off the evergreen trees that stood near our house. The reason I noticed them was because I used to climb up those trees and now that those branches were gone, the trees were way harder to climb! It wasn't until years later that I put two and two together and realized what my dad had done. Dad had cut some branches off the evergreen trees outside our house, and tied them together with twine string, just so we could have a Christmas tree! The thought of that still makes me cry. I realize how poor we were, and how rich we were all at the same time!

Now we move ahead to Christmastime in the early 1970's. It was another bleak year here for my parents. Around the 23rd of December that year, we still didn't have a tree, and hopes for getting one were pretty slim. There just wasn't enough money that year to get one. Things were different in those years. For one thing, credit cards weren't easy to come by, so if a person had no money to get something that was either needed or wanted, you just went without it. In this case, it was the Christmas tree. My Mom said that we should all get together in the kitchen and pray about this situation. Knowing me, I probably just said, "God, get us a tree!" My prayers always seem to be rather simplistic! That evening, Mom and my older sister, Marie, had to go to town for something and when they returned, they had a Christmas tree! My Mom told us, "It was a miracle, that's what it was!" Evidently when Mom and my sister were going to town, a truck loaded with Christmas trees passed them. A tree that was on top of the load flew off and landed in the ditch! The truck never stopped, but my Mom did, and she and my sister stuffed that tree in the back seat of our car! I will always remember that year as the year God gave us a Christmas tree!

I don't remember much more about those two Christmases long ago, but they are stuck in my mind as my two favorite ones, and the lessons they hold for me are priceless!

I do have one more favorite Christmas story, the time I gave my oldest sister, Marie, a frozen weasel, but I will keep that one for another time! I will say this though, it was a real scream!

My next story takes place in 1999. It has nothing to do with Christmas, but everything to do about God's provision! It was midsummer and a drive shaft for a piece of machinery had busted. I took the piece to Smith's Mill Implement, a place where my family has done business since 1941. The parts man at the counter was Leo. Leo got me what I needed, but when I told him to just charge it, Leo said, "I can't, George. You are over your credit limit." "You have to charge the part, Leo, or I'm going to have to write you a bad check," I told him. Leo hurried off to get Pat, one of the owners of the implement place. "What's this about George giving us a bad check?" Pat asked. "I'm going to have to, Pat, if you don't charge the part!" I told him. "There's nothing I can do. You are over your credit limit," said Pat. "What's my credit limit?" I asked, as I didn't think I owed them very much at that point. "One thousand dollars," Pat said. I answered, "Pat, I have owed this place as much as $8000 at one time and you always got your money!" "You charge that part, Pat, or I will go to Mankato where they will!" I said. There were eight other farmers looking straight at Pat when I was talking to him and it was so quiet you could've heard a pin drop in the place! Pat looked at me and he looked at the other farmers and he quietly said "George, you pay for that as soon as you can."

After Christmas that year I had to stop in at Smith's Mill Implement again. This took place on the Friday before New Year's Day. I walked into the implement company and there was Pat behind the counter. Several other folks were in there also. Before Pat could ask me if I was going to pay them something, I asked him, "How much do I owe you guys, Pat?" "Two thousand, six hundred," he said. "OK," I answered, and wrote out a check! Pat looked right at me, held up the check, and asked, "Is this any good?" "All but $600," I said. Once again, you could've heard a pin drop as everyone listened with anticipation. "Why do you always have to do that, George?" Pat asked. A man that was standing behind me spoke up. "The naked truth is better than a dressed up lie!" About this time the whole place filled with roaring laughter! "What are you going to do, George, because I'm going to cash this check," Pat said. "How would I know what I'm going to do, Pat? It would take all the fun out of it if I knew what I was going to do!" I said. The whole place was just busting out with laughter, but I was basing my thoughts and actions on God's word:

Philippians 4:19: *And my God will meet all of your needs according to his glorious riches in Christ Jesus.*

I had the $2000 dollars, but I needed $600 more. If what I was doing (FARMING) was God's will for me to be doing, the repair bill was a need, not a want, I reckoned! Like I mentioned before, this had taken place on a Friday, and a fishing trip was planned for Lake of the Woods with Tim and Terry on Monday. I would be gone for quite a few days when Monday rolled around. Sunday evening came and I was starting to wonder if God was going to act, as it was now 7:30 PM and still no sign that God was going to supply my need! I remember saying a short prayer that went something like "God, if you're going to help me out, we really don't have much time here."

In other words, I was asking God if he could step on it! About ten to fifteen minutes after this prayer, Howard Guse called me. "George," he said "I have a problem!" "Well, join the club!" I said. "I made too much money this year, and I need to get some spent before the New Year to avoid paying taxes. I want to prepay for some hay. When can we get together?" "How about in 20 minutes," I said. I drove over to Howard's, and he gave me a check for $2500 towards hay for the next year. I put the check in the bank the first thing in the morning and went up north fishing with no worries at all! God lived up to his end of the bargain. Even if he didn't give me a a whole lot of time, he did give me what I needed! Like I always say, "Just by the width of a gnat's eyelash!"

The last story that I want to share with you happened in 2003. I like to call it the "Story of the $2 bill". Back in 1976, the US Department of the Treasury started printing $2 bills for our nation's 200th birthday, the Bicentennial Now, the older folks that were around back then had seen $2 dollar bills before, but I had never seen one. They seemed sort of neat to a fourteen year old boy so I started collecting them. Every so often one would come my way and into my cigar box they would go. Over time (27 years, almost to the day), I collected about $200 worth of them. One year in 2003, my nephew, Nate, went to S.E.P. (Spiritual Enhancement Program) summer camp sponsored by my church, Worldwide Church of God. Nate decided that he wanted to be baptized, and he wanted me to do it. This was going to take place on July 4th, 2003. I was to drive down to Camp Abe Lincoln in Buffalo, Iowa, about a six hour drive from here. I didn't have any problem with this except that I had no money for the trip! I prayed and prayed for provision, but none would come. A couple hours before I was to leave, God seemed to be speaking to me, not in a voice that was audible; it was more like a feeling. He said, "George, you already have the provision! Remember your $2 bill collection and how you have been saving it for a special occasion? Well, this is it!" "Oh, no God, not my $2 bill collection! Anything but that! I've been saving it since I was four-teen!" Like God didn't know that! Have you ever found yourself arguing with God? If you have, then you know it generally doesn't do you much good!

So with my $2 bill collection and a jar half full of change, I headed to Buffalo, Iowa at 3:30 a.m. on the 4th of July. Here are a few interesting details about my story. Nate is a twin and he is the second person I have baptized on the 4th of July. All the way down and all the way back, I made ladies that were attending gas stations very happy with my 1976 $2 bills! It seemed as if everyone was collecting them! When I got back home, I didn't have many left. By August, after I had given Nate one and Brad Claggett one, I didn't have the heart to collect them anymore, so I put the last few in the collection plate at church. So much for 27 years of collecting 1976 $2 bills! It was a strange thing, though. That fall during the pumpkin season, I kept finding 1976 $2 bills in my money box on the pumpkin stand, but only in the one here at my place, never at any of the three stands that I had in other locations! I never did keep them though! I would tell people the story I'm telling you now, and give them the $2 bill to remember the story! But one afternoon that fall, I was checking the money box that is on the stand at the end of my driveway. I unlocked the box, and there lying on the top of the pile of money, perfectly straight, was a 1963 $2 bill - not a crease or a wrinkle. It looked brand new! I hollered at Brad to come and look at this sight! Considering the way the small slot in the box is cut, it is absolutely impossible to put paper money in without folding it. It could never be placed so perfectly flat and untouched! God must have put it in there himself! I gave that one to my sister, Jane, because it was the year she was born! I still don't collect them anymore, but every year God sends me a $2 bill from 1976, and a person to tell this story to! So if a $2 bill from 1976 shows up before or after you read this story, I for one <u>would not be surprised</u>! So if you will excuse me now, I kind of have a hankering for another candy cane!

Luke 2:15-20: *When the angels had left them and gone into heaven, the shepherds said to one another, "Let's go to Bethlehem and see this thing that has happened, which the Lord has told us about." So they hurried off and found Mary and Joseph, and the baby, who was lying in the manger. When they had seen him, they spread the word concerning* *what had been told them about this child, and all who heard it were amazed at what the shepherds said to them. But Mary treasured up all these things and pondered them in her heart. The shepherds returned, glorifying and praising God for all the things they had heard and seen, which were just as they were told.*

Merry Christmas and God's peace and abundant blessings to you all!

Your brother in Christ,

George Denn

HEY BY GEORGE!   **January 5, 2008**

Colossians 1: 21-23: *Once you were alienated from God and were enemies in your minds because of your evil behavior. But now he has reconciled you by Christ's physical body through death to present you holy in his sight, without blemish and free from accusation — if you continue in your faith, established and firm, not moved from the hope held out in the gospel. This is the gospel that you heard and that has been proclaimed to every creature under heaven, and of which I Paul have become a servant.*

After I had finished hauling a load of wood the other day, it was getting towards evening. I had just sat down to check my e-mail, because I hadn't checked it for a few days. One of the e-mails I received was from a young friend of mine, Joe Kruse. Joe worked for me this past fall, and stayed at my place this last month. Actually, I had just returned home from Spring Valley, MN around noon that very day. I had driven Joe there to his new home and new job. Just like all the other young men that have helped me over the years here, and then moved on, I had a hard time saying goodbye to Joe! I've never had any sons of my own so I kind of just adopt those that work for me as my (spiritual) sons. Here are a couple of points that I want to share with you from his e-mail. He mentioned that I had helped him in more ways than I would know. Also he mentioned that I should not forget about the time that he drove my Dodge pickup into the wood splitter, scraping the door, and that he owed me one! This does amuse me because anybody that has ever worked for me seems to have smashed my pickup into something (excluding the ladies of course!) I have come to see, however, that over the years there is a force that tries to get between relationships!

2 Corinthians 2:9-11: *The reason I wrote you was to see if you would stand the test and be obedient in everything. If you forgive anyone, I also forgive him. And what I have forgiven - if there was anything to forgive - I have forgiven* *in the sight of Christ for your sake, in order that Satan might not outwit us, for we are not unaware of his schemes.*

So the way that I see it, any of you guys out there that have smashed my pickups are good guys! Also, you are forgiven if I haven't said that to you already. (But I believe I have! But Joe, since you have smashed my good pickup you are a great guy, and you owe me nothing! Friends are a gift from God and they do not keep any records of wrongs; they help one another along life's path! So Joe, I forgive you! God forgives you! And if you bring this up again I am going to flip!

The last day Joe was here, he was packing his things, cleaning out his stuff, and throwing things away that he no longer needed. He even gave his car with a full tank of gas to his younger brother! On top of everything that he had thrown away, I noticed an unopened bag of shelled pumpkin seeds. This small bag of pumpkin seeds was part of his Christmas gift from one of the members of his family. This gift contained other things like hot chocolate, chocolate covered pretzels, homemade soap and various other things. "Joe," I said, "You're throwing away your pumpkin seeds without even trying them!" He told me that they didn't look very appetizing to him. I, on the other hand, know how good they are and rescued them from being thrown away! I was eating them on our way to Spring Valley and shared some with my old friend, Troy. He seemed to like them, too! We were teasing Joe about "judging a book by its cover." I have been thinking about those pumpkin seeds for the past few days now! I was thinking how often we are like that with God's greatest gift to us, his son, Jesus Christ, or some of the smaller aspects that go along with our belief in him! I know I am guilty of tossing them aside, just like my friend Joe did with the pumpkin seeds! So just as I encouraged Joe to try the pumpkin seeds, I encourage you all, as it says in:

Psalm 34:8-9-10: *To taste and see that the Lord is good; blessed is the man who takes refuge in him. Fear the Lord, you his saints, for those who fear him lack nothing. The lions* *may grow weak and hungry, but those who seek the Lord lack no good thing.*

Also I would like you to remember this:

Romans 6:23: *For the wages of sin is death, but the gift of God is eternal life in Christ Jesus our Lord.*

Don't forget to try all that this gift contains for you!

And, Joe Kruse, no matter where this life takes you and what God has in store for you, always remember this - that you, too, have helped me in far more ways than you will ever know!

May God's peace and abundant blessings be with you all!

Your Brother in Christ,

George Denn

HEY BY GEORGE!   **January 17, 2008**

2 Kings 5: 8-10: *When Elisha, the man of God, heard that the king of Israel had torn his robes, he sent him this message: Why have you torn your robes? Have the man come to me and he will know that there is a prophet in Israel. So Naman went with his horses and chariots, and stopped at the door of Elisha's house. Elisha sent a messenger to say to him, "Go wash yourself seven times in the Jordan, and your flesh will be restored and you will be cleansed."*

As you recall, last April I had an incident where a tree whacked me, and I went flying through the air! When I got up off the ground, I knew that my shoulder had been damaged. The pain was worse than you know what! I liked to make a joke out of it, saying that you've heard the saying that "When God gets someone's attention, he slaps them upside the head with a 2x4." Well, with me he uses the whole tree! Having no money at the time and no insurance, going to the doctor was out of the question. I have to admit I have nothing against doctors personally. Even Dr. Luke wrote two books in the Bible! It's the professional end I don't like. Every time I have gone to one, here come the needles full of antibiotics, and every time I get a bill from a doctor, I almost need another doctor! I like to kid my dentist, Bryan, that if I ever do a story about suffering, I'm going to use him as an example! So, Bryan, since this story is not about suffering, you are off the hook!

I am fully convinced that God will heal you in due time if you give him a chance! And yes, he may even use a doctor to do that, too! And, no, I don't believe it is a lack of faith on any one's part if they choose that direction. But you know me, I always have to be different! But one good thing about being different is that it gives me stories to write about, which is pretty important, because I write stories! Well, every chance I could get, I would have people pray for my shoulder. I have had success with prayer for healing in the past, so that was the direction I wanted to go with this injury, also. I would always feel a warmth in my shoulder when people would pray and lay hands on it as they prayed. The shoulder seemed to get better somewhat, but never back to its original state. Also, my muscle had no strength. If I tried to hold my weight, for example, when hanging onto the side of a truck box, unless I used both hands to hang on, I would just fall off! There simply wasn't any strength in that arm! As fall came around, I was wondering how I was going to pick pumpkins with that shoulder. I felt every pumpkin I picked, every bale of hay I tossed, and every piece of fire wood that I handled! By the first of the New Year, I had pretty much made up my mind that I was going to have to live with my shoulder that way the rest of my days. Many times someone would say "You must've tore a muscle or have some deep wound, and you need to go to a doctor for that!" So I reckoned that if God wanted me to go to a doctor for my shoulder, he would also send me some finances so I could do it. Because he didn't provide the means led me to believe that he had another plan!

In the winter months I always try to read through the entire Bible once and the New Testament twice. Since I don't like to work outside in the cold and snow anymore, I figure I have put in my time! Unlike some, I figure it is no wasted time that I do this. Every year there seems to be a theme that God shows me. This year is no different, and here is the theme! Those that listen to God fair pretty well; and those who don't listen to God don't turn out too good! How should I listen to God?

Hebrews 1:1-3: *In the past God spoke to our forefathers through the prophets at many times and in various ways, but in these last days he has spoken to us by his Son, whom he appointed heir of all things, and through whom he made the universe. The Son is the radiance of Gods glory and the exact representation of his being, sustaining all things by his powerful word. After he had provided purification for sins, he sat down at the right hand of the majesty in heaven.*

So if God is in heaven, and Jesus is sitting beside him also, how in the world do we communicate?

John 16:12-15: *Jesus says. I have much more to say to you, more than you can bear. But when he, the Spirit of Truth, comes, he will guide you into all truth. He will not speak on his own; he will speak only what he hears, and will tell you what is yet to come. He will bring glory to me by taking from what is mine and making it known to you. All that belongs to the Father is mine. That is why I said the Spirit will take from what is mine and make it known to you.*

So that's how! You listen to the Holy Spirit! But how do you listen to the Holy Spirit? Sorry, I can't help you there, because everyone is different. I suggest a prayer like this, though. "Father, God, Jesus Christ and Holy Spirit, our great living Lord, please make it so abundantly clear what you want me to do today, and in this situation that I am in. Help me to hear you, help me to see you and heal the parts of my life that are broken, as only you can. In Jesus' name I pray. Amen." And then what happens? Jesus says in Matthew 21:22, *If you believe, you will receive whatever you ask for in prayer.*

Here's what happened to me! For days now I have been praying a prayer similar to the one above. Several days ago, my oldest brother, Wayne, and I had to meet our youngest sister, Jane, at her hair shop "Of the Earth" in Elysian, Minnesota. As usual, Jane was running late and we had an appointment to get to in Albert Lee, Minnesota. As we waited, Jane's associate, Fawn, who does therapeutic message was there. I asked Fawn if she would make an appointment for me to see if she could do something with my shoulder. Jane had mentioned on several occasions that maybe Fawn could help me. I think I just said "Sure, maybe someday." So the appointment was for today at 11:00 a.m. I was in her treatment room for only two minutes when she informed that my shoulder was dislocated. She popped it back into place and "wah-lah", my shoulder was as good as new! She said my muscle would hurt probably for a few days until it got used to being back in place! So today at 11:00 a.m., God decided to provide a healing for my shoulder through a massage therapist named Fawn, an associate of my sister, Jane, in a little shop that they own together called "Of the Earth" in a little town in Minnesota called Elysian, population 486, for a total charge of $0! However, I did leave Fawn a tip. They have a family plan where they work on one another's family members for free.

I had an interesting thought on my way home today from my appointment. Patience is mentioned as one of the fruits of the Holy Spirit in Galatians 6:22, and the people who doctors work on are called "patients" It all just made me laugh!

> **Galatians 6:16, 24-25:** *So I say, live by the Spirit, and you will not gratify the desires of the sinful nature. Those who belong to Christ Jesus have crucified the sinful nature with its passions and desires. Since we live by the Spirit let us keep in step with the Spirit.*

God's peace and abundant blessings to you all!

Your brother in Christ,

George Denn

HEY BY GEORGE! **January 22, 2008**

Ephesians 3:17-18: *So that Christ may dwell in your hearts through faith. And I pray that you, being rooted and established in love, may have power, together with all the saints, to grasp how wide and long and high and deep is the love of Christ, and to know this love that surpasses knowledge- that you may be filled to the measure of all the fullness of God.*

"The Fathers Love" was our theme for Snow Blast 2008 winter camp! Some of us that worked on staff arrived early on Friday evening, January 18th, to be ready for the weekend and the campers. I had been praying to be spiritually prepared for what was to take place this weekend. There wasn't much going on that evening, so Joe and I decided to go back to where he was staying to get his drums, so he would be ready to play them the next evening with the worship team. We were also going to pick up some board games so we'd have something to do. It's about 25 miles to where Joe was staying at our friend, Troy's, place. We were deep into a conversation, about six miles from our destination, with Joe at the wheel. As we went around an icy corner, the car started to slide and we ran into the ditch! One of the problems with this situation was that the car belonged to Troy, who happened to be Joe's boss! Also, it was an extremely cold night, well below zero. I was not dressed as I should have been for the weather! The first thing I told Joe was that we should pray about our predicament. I also told him that it wasn't his fault, that it was purely an accident. I thought that this was an interesting start to Snow Blast, but at the moment, I had a hard time seeing the Father's Love! But I also know that when you are following the Lord, sometimes things are not what they may seem!

Isaiah 55:8-9 *"For my thoughts are not your thoughts, neither are your ways my ways," declares the Lord. "As the heavens are higher than the earth, so are my ways higher than your ways and my thoughts than your thoughts."*

After a couple of hours in the ditch, finally a police officer and a tow truck came to our rescue. We had both left our cell phones back at camp and a fellow that was home on leave from the Army had called 911. As it turned out, my friend, Troy, knew both of these guys and they told us that Troy had taken care of the tow bill! But I did give the tow truck guy a ten dollar bill so he and the police officer could have a warm cup of coffee on me! We had to take the car back to Troy's place because it needed some repair on the back wheel. So we planned to drive Troy's pickup back. However, the pickup battery was dead, and being a diesel, it needed to be plugged in for an hour so that it would start. We got back to Camp Ironwood Springs, which is 25 miles from Joe and Troy's place, at 3:00 a.m. - five hours after we'd left! The only problem was that five miles from camp, Joe said "You will never guess, but I forgot my drumsticks!" We would have to go back, but not tonight! I knew that God had something planned, but I just couldn't see it that night!

The first day of Snow Blast went off without a hitch, *almost*, anyway, as you will see! The campers and the rest of the staff arrived around noon. After a short introduction to camp procedures, the first activity that I took part in was a sleigh ride. Jonathan, the wrangler, told me that he had just gotten the new sleigh about an hour ago and that I was the first one to climb aboard! The temperature was below zero and the horses were real frisky, so we had a pretty good sleigh ride! I tried to talk Richard into going, but he said he had enough sleigh rides for one life time when he was a kid! After the sleigh ride, I took in the snow tubing. Camp Ironwood Springs has the greatest snow tubing hills I've ever been on! Since my youth was spent mostly working, I've have only seen two, though! While snow tubing, I talked with my good friend, Gordy Haack. He told me earlier that while reading my first book, he'd had a hard time because his eyes kept getting moist on him! He also said that I hadn't mentioned him in any of my stories. So I have to say, "I am sorry, Gordy, but I can't mention everybody!"

Later that day, Doug Johannsen taught us how to make peanut brittle, but first I had to start a fire in the fireplace in that building. One of my jobs at camp is to keep fires going or start them. I always start my wood fires back home with a shot of diesel fuel. There are those who like to tease me about this. They would like to believe that I probably can't get a fire going without it, but since I didn't bring any, that is proof that they are wrong! Doug's peanut brittle was pretty tasty, especially with a crackling fire in the fireplace!

Troy and I had to drive back to his place to get Joe's drumsticks and some chess game pieces; also feed his dog and cat. We left around the evening meal time, so I asked Betty to save a couple plates of food for us. Joe was waiting for us when we got back, as the worship service had already begun. But when I handed Joe the drumsticks, he didn't have to say a word - I knew they were the wrong ones! The sticks that I brought were not for the drums he was playing, therefore, they would not work! I told Joe that we would get his drumsticks if I had to go get them myself! So we decided to try again after "dorm chats". (Dorm chats are a time when we older folks take the topic from the day's chapel - in this case "The Father's Love" - and try to have a discussion with the kids in our group. These discussions sometimes can be very interesting!) After dorm chats, I told Joe, "Let's go and get your drumsticks. But first, let's say a prayer before we take off." So we drove the 25 miles to Troy's place, but when we pulled into the yard, we learned that neither of us had brought keys to the house. I had felt pretty confident that this time we would have success, but alas, it was not to be! I just laughed, and said "Now I'm determined to get those drumsticks if it is the last thing that I ever do!" Joe agreed, "Good, so am I!" So we drove back to camp, got the house keys from Troy and this time finally we came back with the drumsticks!

On the way back to camp, I told Joe a story about my past that I had never shared with him. It was the story of how the heartbreak over a girl I once knew eventually led me to the Lord and into the denomination of the Worldwide Church of God! That story had taken around ten years to play itself out! I would not have revealed it to Joe, had we not made so many trips after his drumsticks. Troy also wanted to hear my story, so I promised him I would tell it again at his place the next evening. Well, I was happy that now Joe could use his gift of drum playing in worship to God! And to top it off, I got to bed at 11:30 p.m.!

My good friend, Bob Bardwell, who runs Ironwood Springs Christian Ranch, has a slogan on one of his cards. It says, "Perseverance - A race is not run with the wheels but with the heart!" Bob is in a wheelchair and he has run many a race using one! Many times in the past few years since I met Bob, his slogan has kept me moving forward!

The second day, I took in a Christian living class that David Fiedler was hosting. I thought it interesting that most of the scriptures we looked at that day were the same ones that I'd used in the stories I wrote during the past month! The Holy Spirit was really working there at the camp! It was fascinating trying to take it all in!

Doug's message on the second day was "They never knew the Father's love." One of the things Doug talked about was how God loves to party and how he likes to see his children have fun in church and in worship! I wish my Dad could've understood that 40 years ago. If he did, he probably wouldn't have pulled my ear so many times, telling me to behave myself! One of the scriptures Doug had used was from Luke 15:11-31, the story of the prodigal son (or the "lost son", as my translation calls him.) In that story, the only one the father wished would behave himself was the son that always felt he had! At the end of Doug's message, he asked the question "What do you think happened to the older son who got mad at his father for celebrating the prodigal brother's return?" Since we are supposed to have fun with our worship, this is the way I think he ended up: Personally, I think that fellow ran away to Minnesota and started raising pumpkins, and by seeing all the joy in people who bought pumpkins from him, he finally saw the depth of the Father's love!

I just wanted to add that Joe was finally able to play his drums with the worship team, Jake, the guitar player, and Sharon the worship leader. As I listened to the music, I felt that whatever we'd gone through to get his drumsticks was well worth it! We all would have missed out if we hadn't done all it took to get the tools of his gift there!

Of course, some of my favorite camp activities were breakfast, lunch and dinner; or if you talk like me, dinner and supper! After dinner/supper, Troy Miesner led a Christian living class discussing the "Trinity - Father, Son and Holy Spirit." He asked the question, "What do they do?" His answer: "Trying to accomplish in us and all people to believe in him, and therefore be saved!" He talked about the roles that each one played in this. God, the Father, is the creator. Jesus, the Son, frees us from sin by being sacrificed on the cross. And the Holy Spirit enters our heart, helps us to believe, and leads us into all truth! I have to admit I fell asleep during Troy's message, but like I always say, my eyes may be closed, but my ears are not!

After the class, I got myself into a high stakes poker game, "Texas Hold 'Em". But I didn't last very long, since I lost all my chips in the first hand. In the second hand, I borrowed some chips from a young fellow by the name of David, from Orr, MN. After I lost all my chips again on the second hand, I had to quit because no one would give me anymore! So it is a good thing that I don't gamble for real. I used to, but now you can see why I don't anymore! That's the way I approach everything in life, I guess. It's all the way or not at all!

That afternoon's itinerary included a time slot for sleigh riding, along with the note "Fees apply." I read it wrong and thought it said "Free apples." So as you can guess, I took a lot of kidding for that!

And now it is time to meet those in my dorm. Our gang included Shawn, Joshua, Lium, Sam, Hunter, Jacob, David, Evan, Ian, Coulter, Josh, Tom K., Mike H., Troy M., Joe K., Richard S., a guy named Floyd, and myself. In dorm chats on the last evening, we talked about what we'd learned that morning about our Triune God. Todd Fox had given the final message at chapel that summarized all that we'd heard the past few days. One thing I felt as Snow Blast came to a close was that I sure met a lot of new friends this weekend. And with the friends that I already knew, our friendships became deeper. I also felt that this Snow Blast camp was the best one I'd ever attended! For some reason, this one touched me the most!

After camp, I got to hang out with Joe and Troy at their place, which is about eight miles northeast of Spring Valley, MN. Joe beat me at chess, but then it's been almost thirty years since I played, so I figured I was a little rusty! We watched a couple of movies, had supper together and played a game of dominoes. As we played dominoes, I was able to tell Troy my story of how I'd ended up in the same church as him! Joe had heard some of this story on the last trip we made to get his drum sticks. So maybe there was a reason in God's plan for all of those trips, after all! I also left Troy with a couple copies of my book - one for Mike, the policeman, and one for the tow truck driver who pulled us out of the ditch that first evening. So who knows what God was up to with us this past weekend? This song kept running through my head before I went to camp on Friday and all the way home from Spring Valley on Tuesday.

HOW DEEP THE FATHER'S LOVE FOR US

How deep the Father's love for us,
How vast beyond all measure,
That he should give his only Son
To make a wretch his treasure.

How great the pain of searing loss;
The Father turns his face away,
As wounds which mar the Chosen One
Bring many sons to glory.

Behold, the man upon a cross,
My sin upon His shoulders;
Ashamed, I hear my mocking voice
Call out among the scoffers.

It was my sin that held him there
Until it was accomplished;
His dying breath has brought me life;
I know that it is finished.
I will not boast in anything;
No gifts, no power, no wisdom;
But I will boast in Jesus Christ,
His death and resurrection.

Why should I gain from His reward?
I cannot give an answer;
But this I know with all my heart,
His wounds have paid my ransom.

God's peace and abundant blessings to you all!

Your brother in Christ,

George Denn

HEY BY GEORGE!   **February 8, 2008**

Ecclesiastes 3: 1-8: *There is a time for everything, and a season for every activity under heaven; A time to be born and a time to die, a time to plant and a time to up root, a time to kill and a time to heal, a time to tear down and a time to build, a time to weep and a time to laugh, a time to mourn and a time to dance, a time to scatter stones and a time to gather them, a time to embrace and a time to refrain, a time to search and a time to give up, a time to keep and a time to throw away, a time to tear and a time to mend, a time to be silent and a time to speak, a time to love and a time to hate, a time for war and a time for peace.*

I was reading that scripture yesterday and just had to laugh! I was thinking if wise old Solomon had been from rural Minnesota, he probably would've added a couple more phrases! They probably would have said something like this. "There is a time to cut fire wood and a time to refrain from cutting fire wood; there is a time to go fishing, and the more that you don't cut firewood, the more you can go fishing!" I hope you all can appreciate my humor, because in my life, these two things seem to be a reality. It is now a time to refrain from cutting firewood in my life, and I hope to keep it that way as much as I possibly can! You will understand why I was a little taken aback, so to speak, when my friend, Wayne Schwartz, called me about two weeks ago. Wayne asked if I would come over to his farm and cut down a rather large tree for him. He needed the tree to fall in a certain direction, so he wanted an expert to saw the tree down! I am sure there are a score of others that are far better with a chain saw than I am. And if a couple of my former hired guys could've overheard our conversation, they no doubt would've broken out with hearty laughter, plus would've interjected some fine tales of my lumberjack days when they worked with me in the woods! But those will have to wait for another time! Brad Scholl was the last guy who was brave enough to ask me if I would help him cut wood. I ended up handing him my chainsaw and a pail full of sharp chains, and told him that was all the help he was going to get from me! So now I had to call Brad ask him to bring my saw and chains back because I needed them again. Wayne's convincing me to help him cut this tree had to be an act of God, because at this point in my life, the only thing I dislike more than cutting wood, is cutting wood in the winter time! Now for all you folks that rely on wood heat (like my friends Brad and Wayne), I suggest you take some time in the spring or fall to get this chore done!

I have a chilling tale from the winter of 1978 to share with you. I also have to live out the rest of my days with the effects of frost-bitten hands and feet from that severely harsh winter, because we had no wood on hand except what we could cut on weekends! This turned into a full time job just cutting enough wood to last until the next weekend! Anyway, when I got to Wayne's farm, it was almost noon (or dinner time, for those who talk like me.) Somehow we got into a discussion on several Bible topics. I was reading a few things from his Bible to Wayne and his sons, Peter and Paul. Now, Wayne and I differ on some of our viewpoints. I once belonged to the same church denomination as Wayne, so I can understand where he is coming from. But the Bible tells us not to pass judgment on disputable matters in Romans 14:1. One thing we both can agree on is that it takes the body and blood of Jesus Christ to atone for our sins, and our belief in him is what gives us eternal life.

John 3:16: *For God so loved the world that he gave his one and only Son, that whoever believes in him shall not perish, but have eternal life.*

After our discussion, we came to see that we need to concentrate on what we agree on and not what we disagree on, because what we disagree on has no bearing on salvation, anyway! After dinner, we headed to the woods. I rode behind the tractor in an old manure spreader that Wayne uses for hauling wood, just like my Dad did. It must've been more than 30 years since I'd gone to the woods in a rig like that! One of the highlights of the afternoon was being able to tease Paul, Wayne's youngest son. He was age 14 at the time of this story, and I had a feeling he liked to "give me the business" as well as I liked to give it to him! I sawed the tree down. Let's just say it almost went in the desired direction, and it only knocked a few branches off the tree that Wayne was trying to save! We just looked at each other and laughed - so much for expertise! As I rode back to the farmyard on top of that load of wood, I couldn't help but feel that there was something more to that day than just an afternoon of wood cutting!

About ten days went by, and Wayne stopped by to pay me for the rest of the hay that he owed. Wayne and I have devised a plan to finance each other so we don't need to deal with the banks! I finance him, he finances me. I believe this to be a biblical concept! "Funny thing," he said "my milk check came a week early this time. It is the first time that's happened! That in itself is a miracle, because all the years I milked cows, all the years my Dad milked cows, and all the years my Grandpa milked cows, the milk check never came a week early! It may have come a week late, but never a week early!" While Wayne was at my house he was also able to fix my LP heater. The thing ran for 25 years and finally quit the day before Wayne stopped in! Also, Wayne told me that our conversation the other day had sparked his interest in reading his Bible again! But this time he said he was going to start in the New Testament. I was happy to hear that! I heard it said once that it takes the average person 72 hours to read through the entire Bible. It's such a short time when one looks at a lifetime, but yet so few take the time to read about and come to know the God that loves them more than any human ever could - the one who gave them the very life they live in the first place! How many have squandered their life without ever coming to know the purpose they were created for? I asked Wayne what I owed him for fixing my heater. "Nothing," he said. "Just come over sometime and help me cut wood!"

Ecclesiastes 3:9-15: `*What does the worker gain from his toil? I have seen the burden God has laid on men. He has made everything beautiful in its time. He has also set eternity in the hearts of men; yet they cannot fathom what God has done from the beginning to the end. I know that there is nothing better for men than to be happy and to do good while they live. That everyone may eat and drink, and find* *satisfaction in all his toil - this is a gift of God. I know that everything God does will endure forever; nothing can be added to it and nothing taken from it. God does it so that men will revere him. Whatever is has already been, and what will be has been before; and God will bring the past to account.*

So with the wood cutting behind me, I was looking forward to my next adventure! My friend, Tom Kennebeck, from Orr, MN had arranged our third annual men's fishing retreat. It was to be held on the weekend of February 1-3 on Pelican Lake in Orr, MN. Last fall when Brad was up from Oklahoma, he told me that I should let him know if we were going to have one of these events, so I did. Troy Peterson also told me that he wanted to go if we were having one this year. I asked my friend, Jeff, but he said he couldn't make it on a weekend, as he had used up all his available days. I also asked my friend, Joe Kruse, if he would like to go. I especially wanted to take Joe to meet my friend, Tom Burnett, and to see the log cabin he had built on the southwestern edge of Pelican Lake. One week before the trip, Brad let me know that it was looking pretty impossible for him to go on this trip. I prayed for Brad, hoping that somehow God would make it possible for him to go, but I guess it wasn't meant to be.

I was in Wal-Mart one day getting some fishing supplies, when I received a call on my cell phone from Lisa, one of the ladies that work at Community Bank in the Hy-Vee grocery store in upper Mankato. They were having their Grand Opening with a ribbon cutting ceremony, and the pastor that they had lined up had to bow out at the last minute! Lisa asked me if by chance I might know a pastor. I heard this on my answering service because I didn't want to be talking in the store! I just laughed when I heard the message. Do I know a pastor? Is the Pope Catholic? My best friend, Jeff, is a pastor! I stopped over at the bank and gave Jeff's phone numbers to Lisa. I called him later that day to see if he took the "Bank Job"! He said that he did, and that it was an incredible answer to prayer - something that he would explain later!

Troy Peterson showed up that evening, only to let me know that he could no longer go on the trip, either. I prayed for Troy, but his going on this trip was not meant to be either. I remember being disappointed, but at the same time knowing that God always brings together everyone that needs to be there! I thought "Boy, I hope Joe doesn't back out or I'll have to go by myself!" Joe called later that day and said that I should come down to get him around 6:30 p.m. the next evening. On the way down to get Joe, I called Jeff to find out how praying for the bank went. We talked for practically the whole trip down to Spring Valley, about an hour or so! We talked about so many things that were going on in our lives. One of the things Jeff told me was that the whole "Bank Job" was an answer to a prayer, and he wouldn't tell me any more about it until I got home from the fishing trip! As I drove into Spring Valley, I told Jeff I had to go - my mouth was drier than the Sahara Desert and I needed something to drink! Well, I got to Troy's house; Joe and Troy were cooking supper. I had to tell Joe that it looked like it was just going to be him and me on this trip.

We came back to my place that evening. The next morning, I had to haul a load of wood, so Joe went to visit his parents. Shortly after Joe got back, we took off for Orr. But I forgot to stop my mail, so we had to drive back about seven miles to the post office to do that. We stopped at my friend, Gordy's, for a few minutes to pick up his portable fish house and heater. Gordy lives west of Duluth. I was sort of thinking that maybe we should take his power ice auger too, but Tom said he had that taken care of! When we pulled into Orr, I was wondering where I would have to look for Tom Kennebeck. But as I pulled into town, there he was filling his jeep up with gas at the bait shop, right before you come to the traffic light! Tom saw us first and was waving at us. When we pulled in behind him, he said he was just wondering where we would meet, and he just looked up and there we were!

One of the first things I noticed was talk of how depressed the economy was in town, a theme that would be repeated often during our trip. Orr relies heavily on the fishing and tourism trade, and mainly snowmobiles in the winter. This year it was just not happening! I strongly feel that God is allowing this condition for a reason, maybe to get the citizens of Orr to look to Him for answers instead of looking to money for all the solutions! Tom was showing us his old minnow pail when suddenly the handle broke and minnows went flying out all over the ground! Tom said he ended up spending $50 on gas and minnows. I told Tom that by the sound of things in the bait shop, I doubted if they minded!

After we got settled in the place where we were staying for the next couple days, we had chili for supper. Then Mitch and Simie Kennebeck, Tom's son and daughter-in-law, showed up with Ezra, their 15 month old son and a friend, John, who was 16. Simie had made some Amish friendship bread. I have heard of it, but it was the first time I got to eat any. Boy, was it good! Then we all got into a game of dominos. This set had double 15's and we played Mexican Train. It took us three hours just to play three rounds! Sometime after 9:00 p.m., who should show up but Anthony Bisbee! Anthony was at our fishing retreat last year, and I hadn't seen him since then. Anthony is the same age as Joe, 21, so I'm glad they got to meet each other. Last year, Anthony told us that he was buying a trenching machine to put in electric wires. So I was curious about how his year went. He said it was far different than he imagined it would be. Let's just say it was an adventure! We had to say goodbye to Anthony a short time later. He had to work the next day so he couldn't join us for fishing. I've known Anthony for six years now. It was sure good to see him again, and I hated to say goodbye, but I know someday, God willing, we will meet again! After some prayer time I went to bed. I think Joe and Tom stayed up for a while talking, but I was tired!

Our fishing morning started with breakfast. I fried pancakes while Tom cooked eggs and sausage. I don't think Joe cooked anything that day, but he washed some dishes. As I fried the pancakes, the griddle that I used smoked a little bit. So I was teased about the house being foggy! It seems that ribbing one another is half the fun on these trips! After breakfast we decided to check out our fish house that we were going to use. We had to walk, because the snow was too deep to drive through that year. About half way out to the ice house, I almost wished I'd taken Gordy up on his offer to borrow his snowmobile as well! We got out to the ice house, and all that was out there was an ice chisel. So Tom started chiseling a hole with that. He almost had gone three feet deep when I took over chopping. I bet I hadn't chopped five times with the thing when, splosh, it went through the ice out of my hands, through the hole and into Davey Jones locker - in other words, the bottom of Pelican Lake! I told Tom that we may as well all go back and find an ice auger, because we couldn't fish without any holes cut! Tom had to stop and do something at the place he works, but it wasn't going to take him long. While Joe and I waited for Tom,we got into a game of Tic Tac Toe. I was ahead for a while, but Joe won in the end. Then we played two games of hangman. Joe won that, too! I guess I'm no good at games. Tom arrived, carrying his own ice auger. This time we took Gordy's portable ice house with us. Joe and I dragged it out there like a sled, just in case someone else came out to fish. No one came! Tom's ice auger was extremely dull, but he did manage to get a couple of holes opened up for Joe and I to start fishing. Tom also stated that now he remembered why he didn't use his ice auger any more! I gave Tom a $100 bill, telling him to go into town and get us an ice auger that would work. Tom returned with an auger that belonged to the guy that owns the place where we were staying. Apparently the person he was counting on to provide us with a power ice auger was gone and the auger was laying in pieces on the guy's basement floor! We all had a good laugh! It's a good thing that fishing isn't the main thing on these fishing retreats! After Tom drilled his hole and sat down to fish, we heard this power ice auger start up about 500 feet away from us! Once again we all just laughed!

I shared with the guys that I had been baptized on February 29th, 1996, and that this was a leap year, also! I distinctly remember my pastor at the time, Charles Holladay, saying," Jeez, George, not many people get baptized on the 29th of February!" I also remember coming up out of that very cold water, truly knowing that Jesus really had forgiven any sin I had committed, was committing or would commit! It was an experience I shall never forget! Since Joe talked mainly about his upcoming trip to Italy (and possibly Africa and China), Tom and I prayed for his trip.

I did catch one fish that day. Tom's son, Mitch, took a picture of it, and I filleted it when we got back to the house. On our way to the AmericInn hotel, where we were eating that night, we stopped to see a guy that Tom knows, named Bill. He built a house on a hill, so Tom calls him "Bill on the Hill"! Meeting Bill and seeing his new house was quite a thrill, especially when it came time to leave. Tom had to open the back door on his Jeep so he could see to back down the hill! And I suppose there isn't much sense in mentioning the cougar Bill has prowling around his place, because people from around here would think I may be stretching things a bit! I enjoyed our meeting Bill and hope to meet him again someday. He has been going to Tom's church, so we did get to see him again on Sunday. After our meeting with Bill, Tom took Joe past the Catholic church so that he'd know where it was in the morning.

Tom's son, Chris, cooked our walleye sandwiches at the dining room at the AmericInn. Afterwards, did that hot tub ever feel good! Mitch took some pictures of us coming out of the water slide. I always wonder where all this fun stuff was when I was kid! It sure would have been a whole lot more fun than the axe handles and pitch forks we used, that's for sure! We ended the evening watching a movie, National Treasure. After a time of prayer, another day of our fishing retreat had ended.

After breakfast on Sunday, we loaded our stuff, because our time here had ended. Joe went to Mass at Holy Cross Catholic Church while Tom and I started setting up for our church service that started at 11:00 a.m. Joe joined us after mass was over. When Communion time came, I helped Tom move the Communion table to the center of the room and we all gathered around it to partake of the elements. Later we learned that the evening before, Joe and Tom were talking, and evidently Joe said something that struck Tom as being very profound, so profound that it moved Tom to position the table *among* us! It was at that moment I knew God had used Joe to touch us all! After a lunch with the church group, it was time to say goodbye to Tom, Mitch, Ezra, Bill on the hill and all the others. It is just so hard to say goodbye to all of those people that I have now come to love as family!

Joe and I drove out to see Tom and Jenny Burnett and family. I wanted Joe to meet Tom and to hear his story, and to see the log cabin he had built on his property next to the lake. I hadn't seen Tom and Jenny for over a year, and it sure was good to see them again! Tom, Joe, and I prayed for a mutual friend that was going through some marriage problems. Tom and Jenny are living examples of how a lost cause wasn't a lost cause when God decided to heal their marriage! The afternoon just seemed to fly by and once again it was hard to say goodbye to Tom and Jenny, but we had to. We drove the two hours back to Gordy and Bonnie's home for supper and spent the evening there. After supper, I was pretty wiped out. Gordy and Joe stayed up and watched the Super Bowl and talked for awhile, but since I'm not a sports fan, I went to bed.

The next morning before breakfast, Gordy's friend, Moose, called. Gordy put Moose on the speaker phone and it was as if he was right there among us! On a sad note, Gordy told me that Geno, Gordy's brother-in-law, had been diagnosed with Lou Gehrig's disease. I had just met Geno last year. I was glad to have met him, and the news saddened me. After breakfast it was time to say goodbye to Gordy and Bonnie. I realized on the way home pretty soon it would be time to say goodbye to Joe and our fishing retreat would be over. Good Lord, how I hate goodbyes!

On our drive back home, we saw three interesting things. First, we saw a raven, which to some is a sign of death! Next, we saw a car wipe out right in front of us. Thankfully, no one got hurt. It just hit some ice and spun out of everyone's way! The road was very slippery in spots, but you couldn't tell by the appearance of the road! I sure was glad that Gordy prayed for travel mercies for us! We also saw a Bald Eagle, which represents freedom! Joe and I stopped and bought a few things for supper to go with our fish. We also got several movies to watch for the evening. Joe bought "St. Therese", and I bought "The Five People You Meet in Heaven" and "A River Runs Through It". After breakfast in the morning, it was time to say goodbye to Joe. It was all I could do to keep from crying. There are those who like to say I'm just getting soft in my old age! But I say it is just hard to say goodbye to those you have come to love as family! On my way home I thought fondly of all the people I got to see this weekend that have become special in my life: Tom Kennebeck, Mitch, Simie, and Ezra Kennebeck and their friend, John, Chris Kennebeck, others at Tom's church, Anthony Bisbee, Tom and Jenny Burnett, Gordy and Bonnie Lindquist, and

Joe Kruse. I started humming this hymn that I used to sing back when I was a worship leader at church:

GOD BE WITH YOU!

Verse 1: God be with you till we meet again;
By his counsel's guide, uphold you;
With his sheep securely fold you;
God be with you till we meet again.
Chorus: Till we meet—Till we meet, Till we meet at Jesus feet;
Till we meet—Till we meet,
God be with you till we meet again
Verse 2: God be with you till we meet again;
Neath his wings protecting hide you;
Daily manna still provide you;
God be with you till we meet again.
Chorus
Verse 3: God be with you till we meet again;
When life's perils thick confound you
Put his arms unfailing round you;
God be with you till we meet again.
Chorus
Verse 4: God be with you till we meet again;
Keep love's banner floating o'er you;
Smite death's threat'ning wave before you;
God be with you till we meet again.
Chorus

When I got home that day I noticed something strange! There was a sack of potatoes next to my coffee pot. I couldn't remember buying them nor placing them there! Later my friend, Jeff, called while he was in town. I told him to stop out and tell me the rest of his story that he couldn't tell me about until I got home, about the "Bank Job". The first thing he did when he arrived was open my refrigerator door. It was full of food! Here is his story in full.

The other morning, Jeff was driving by my place, and he commented to God that George's refrigerator never seems to have much food in it! He asked God, if it was his will, to provide the means so he could buy me some groceries. Somewhere about that time, Lisa from Community Bank at Hy-Vee in Mankato called my cell phone, wondering if I would happen to know a pastor that could pray for their Grand Opening, as the one that they had lined up was now unable to do it! I was at Wal-Mart when the call came, so I drove over to the bank, and gave Lisa Jeff's phone numbers. Lisa called Jeff to see if he would do this. Lisa also mentioned to Jeff that this was the first time she had been involved with something of this nature! Jeff was to read Proverbs 3:5-6 on the day of the Grand Opening. That scripture reads as follows: *"Trust in the Lord with all of your heart and lean not on your own understanding. In all your ways acknowledge him and he will make your paths straight."*

Jeff was also to say a prayer that day for the bank. For all of this, he received a $50 gift certificate to Hy-Vee. So God gave him the means that he asked for, and bought me a bunch of groceries! "Isn't that a corker!" (as my Grandpa Denn used to say!)

Colossians 1:15-23: He is the image of the invisible God, the first born over all creation. For by him all things were created; things in heaven and on earth, visible and invisible, whether thrones or powers or rulers or authorities, all things were created by him and for him. He is before all things, and in him all things hold together. And he is head of the body, the church; he is the beginning and the first born from among the dead, so that in everything he might have the supremacy. For God was pleased to have all his fullness dwell in him, and through him to reconcile to himself all things, whether things on earth or things in heaven, by making peace through his blood, shed on the cross. Once you were alienated from God and were enemies in your minds because of your evil behavior. But now he has reconciled you by Christ's physical body through death to present you holy in his sight, without blemish and free from accusation if you continue in your faith, established and firm, not moved from the hope held out in the gospel. This is the gospel that you heard and that has been proclaimed to every creature under heaven and of which I, Paul have become a servant.

God's peace and abundant blessings and happy fishing to you all!

Your brother in Christ,

George Denn

HEY BY GEORGE!   **February 20, 2008**

Psalm 139:1-18: O Lord, you have searched me and you know me. You know when I sit and when I rise; you perceive my thoughts from afar. You discern my going out and my lying down; you are familiar with all my ways. Before a word is on my tongue, you know it completely, O Lord. You hem me in-behind and before; you have laid your hand upon me. Such knowledge is too wonderful for me, too lofty for me to attain. Where can I go from your Spirit? Where can I flee from your presence? If I go up to the heavens, you are there; if I make my bed in the depths, you are there. If I rise on the wings of the dawn, if I settle on the far side of the sea, even there your hand will guide me; your right hand will hold me fast. If I say, "Surely the darkness will hide me and the light become night around me," even the darkness will not be dark to you; the night will shine like the day, for darkness is as light to you. For you created my innermost being; you knit me together in my mother's womb. I praise you because I am fearfully and wonderfully made; your works are wonderful, I know that full well. My frame was not hidden from you when I was made in the secret place. When I was woven together in the depths of the earth, your eyes saw my unformed body. All the days ordained for me were written in your book before one of them came to be. How precious to me are your thoughts, O God! How vast the sum of them! Were I to count them, they would outnumber the grains of sand. When I awake I am still with you.

Psalm 139:23-24: Search me, O God, and know my heart; test me and know my anxious thoughts. See if there is any offensive way in me, and lead me in the way everlasting.

As I write this story, I am sitting in a recliner at the house of my sister, Marie, and her husband, Les, in Redmond, Oregon. I am visiting out here with my Dad for about a week. It's been about 60 degrees the past few days and if I want to see snow, I have to look at the mountains! Just a week ago, my friend, Jeff, and I were ice fishing with Gordy and Moose near Duluth, MN where the ice is three feet thick on the lakes! We had a great time, even if we didn't catch any fish! We got my pickup stuck once, but we did come home with a real nice four-man portable fish house that we didn't have when we went up - total cost: $0. How is that for provision from the Lord! As I was getting ready to come out to Oregon, Brad Scholl called me. He needed some more firewood. I told Brad that he had made it into my last story! Brad laughed and asked if I told how he traded me wood for straw! Now I have to try and turn the straw into money! Wasn't there a story written about a person who did that? I think it was about a girl with a funny name and she had longer hair and lived in a better house than I have! The only problem is that this is no fairy tale!

The last time I was away from home, some snow must have blown into one of my chimneys, and one of my wood stoves wasn't drawing right so I kept getting smoked out; all the more reason to go somewhere else for a while! Troy Peterson and his brother-in-law, Kenyon, took Dad and me to the airport in Minneapolis. On our way, we had some laughs! I told them about this dream I had a couple of years ago. In my dream, I was walking and came to two rivers that were side by side with a small amount of land in between them. The rivers were both frozen over, so I walked across the first river and spent the night on the other side. In the morning, I noticed that the river I had crossed the day before had broken up, and it was now full of ice chunks. All along shore and in between the chunks of ice, I could see fish - lots of them, all the same kind, and all the same size! After I saw this, I turned and walked across the strip of land that was in between the rivers. The second river hadn't broken up and I started walking across it, but as I walked across, I noticed the ice was starting to melt because it was getting warmer out. I realized that the ice was melting very rapidly under my feet, so I started to run. I was running, but the ice was melting faster than I could run and I had to leap towards the shore. I don't know if I made it or not, as my dream ended there! One interesting thing about my life is that I was baptized on February 29, 1996. It was a Leap Year, as is February 2008. For some reason I have a feeling that this has some significance to my dream. I'm not going to say that dreams have any meanings to them, because I feel most of them don't. However when they are as vivid as this one, and I can remember them for years as I can this one, they make me wonder "Is God trying to tell me something?" The Bible does mention that God sometimes speaks to men in this way.

> **Job 33:14-18:** For God does speak - now one way, now another - though man may not perceive it. In a dream, in a vision of the night, when deep sleep falls on men as they slumber in their beds, he may speak in their ears and terrify them with warnings, to turn man from wrong doing and keep him from pride, to preserve his soul from the pit, his life from perishing from the sword.

So I am still out on dreams and what they mean, if anything at all. Kenyon had a dream, too, that he shared, but I will let him tell it if he wants to, because if I did, I would have had to change his name!

We said goodbye to Troy and Kenyon, went to the ticket counter, checked our luggage, and went though the line where they search you to make sure you're not carrying a weapon. I got buzzed because I forgot to take my cell phone out of my pocket. Once we got through, all we had to do was find our gate C16 and wait for our plane. I brought a book along that my friend, Terry, had given me to read - something about being between a rock and a hard place! When I saw the title, I just laughed and asked myself "Why do I have to read a book like that? My life is full of experiences of that nature!" The book helped me to kill some time and for the most part I agreed with the author. But a few things we didn't see eye to eye on, but then what else is new? We flew from Minneapolis to Seattle, Washington, then changed planes and flew to Redmond, Oregon, about a 1300 mile trip. While we were flying, I sat on the right side of the plane. The wing of the plane was just outside my window. Every once in a while I would see the wing shake a little, and see the plane engine vibrate a bit. They reminded me of the exhaust pipe on my tractor, but I just hoped they didn't break off like I've seen the exhaust pipe do a time or two! As I was flying, I thought of my Great, Great Grandpa Jacob Peter Denn. He came out to Oregon in 1892 and settled in the Camas Valley, twenty miles west of the town of Roseburg, Oregon. In the total flight time of 4.5 hours, we were going the same distance as it took him a week to travel coming out here by train!

The morning after we arrived, the plan was to drive across the Cascade Mountains to the west coast to see the Pacific Ocean, then go south to Camas Valley where my ancestors settled, then to Roseburg, then back to Redmond. So in the morning, we took off towards the mountains. My brother-in-law, Les, drove us nimbly down the mountain pass for about 100 miles. Half way across the mountains, there was a pickup truck and trailer with the word ABBA written in huge letters across the back window of the pickup! Romans 8:15-16 mentions this name.

For you did not receive a spirit that makes you a slave again to fear, but you received the Spirit of sonship. And by him we cry "Abba, Father." The Spirit himself testifies with our spirit that we are God's children.

Also it is mentioned in Galatians 4:6-7

Because you are sons, God sent the Spirit of his Son into our hearts, the Spirit who calls out,"Abba, Father." So you are no longer a slave, but a son; and since you are a son, God has made you also an heir.

Shortly after we came upon this vehicle, he pulled over to let us pass, then immediately pulled back in behind us. I thought how God does the same - he goes before us and behind us! When we reached the other side of the mountains, it looked like early May in Minnesota! The one thing I didn't like about being there was I knew that I'd have spring fever when I got back home, since it was 60 degrees in Oregon and below -0 back in Minnesota! We drove into the town of Florence and there it was - the Pacific Ocean! I walked down across some rocks and stuck my hand in the water. I sort of laughed because when my nephew, Dustin, was younger, he used to tell me that I needed to be more Pacific! (He meant I needed to be more specific.) So now I can tell Dustin that I am more Pacific!

While I was climbing back up the rocks, my cell phone started to ring. It was Howard Guse from back home. I said, "Howard, you'll never guess what I am doing right now!" Howard said, "Knowing you George, that would be hard to tell!" I told Howard that I was looking out across the Pacific Ocean. I don't know why, but Howard seemed pretty impressed by that! A short time later we called my sister, Jane. My nephew, Dustin, is her son. We all laughed and told her that she could inform Dustin that finally we now are all more Pacific! Afterwards, we traveled south to Coos Bay, and then east to Camas Valley. It was said that my Great, Great Grandfather Jacob Peter Denn had bought 3000 acres in that valley 116 years ago. But by the looks of things, it had long since been sold off into smaller parcels. Still, it was interesting to see the very spot I have heard so much about in stories growing up. It wasn't anything like I had imagined it! There was a street in Roseburg called Denn Ave. So we found the street and Dad, Marie and I had Les take our picture underneath the street sign! Jacob Peter Denn came back to Minnesota around 1912. He died at the home of his son, Paul Denn (my Great Grandpa) on November 22, 1914 and is buried in St. Clair, MN at the Catholic cemetery.

One evening we had the opportunity to have a tour of the place where my sister works, Whispering Winds Retirement Center. While waiting for Marie to finish her cleaning on the third floor, Les, Dad and I introduced ourselves to the two ladies at the front desk, Linda Hines and Sally Limbeck. Sally had purchased three of my books so I was able to sign them for her. We were told to go over to a side room and have some coffee, and there we met Stephanie Adams. Marie came and showed us around some, and then we had supper with all the residents. We were introduced to a whole bunch of people that my sister cleans for up on the third floor. Last May, I was sad to see my sister leave Minnesota. But know I can see God has placed her here to minister to all these neat senior citizens! I told Marie that there is no way she would ever be able to quit working here now, the way everyone just loves her. They wouldn't let her if she wanted too! I talked to a lady named Emily She was originally from Montgomery, MN. We talked about a little town north of Montgomery called Heidelberg. I thought it was interesting - here I was 1300 miles away from home and I was talking to somebody about a little town in Minnesota that probably doesn't have 100 people living there! It sure was a great blessing to meet all the folks that either live or work at Whispering Winds in Bend Oregon!

One thing I notice most around here is all the rocks and stones that lay on top of the ground. I told Dad that it reminded me of that piece of ground that we used to farm over by the hills near Elysian, MN. As I recall, Dad and I were over there picking up rocks to get the ground ready for planting corn. Every time we worked the ground we had to pick up the stones. After about three days of rock picking, I'd had enough! I walked over to where Dad was and told him that if we didn't stop picking up the stones, there wasn't going to be any more ground left to farm! I asked Dad if he remembered that; he said he did and we all just laughed! Today we went out to a place where they raise pumpkins. Everything here has to be irrigated. We also went to see a place called Smith Rock. What a breath taking place! As my week out here in Oregon comes to an end, I can say I am glad to have had the chance to visit, but the place that God has placed me for ministry is on my farm back in Minnesota! It sure was a great flight back to Minnesota, crossing the mountains and being above the clouds. I sure like to fly!

As my plane started to descend into Minneapolis, I don't even know why I thought of it, but my mind started to wander back in time to summers long ago, baling countless loads of hay with Grandpa Denn, Uncle Lowell, Dad, brothers and cousins. I would lie on top of those loads of hay while they made their way to the end of the field or one of the three barns that needed to be filled. As the hay rack rocked back and forth, I would look up at the clouds and wonder what it would be like to be above them! The plane was dark, so no one could see me crying as the memories of those long ago days passed through my mind. It is kind of funny now, but looking down at those clouds, there isn't nearly the work involved that there was when I could only wonder what it was like above them! For years now I have made this statement that my farm is the only place in the world where I can be myself and get by with it! My friend, Joe Kruse, is the only person so far to challenge me on that statement. A couple months ago he told me that he didn't know if that was true or not, but if it was true, then the farm was a good place to be! My farm is a great place to be; it is where my ministry is! And as always when I return there, usually the first place I go is to the house!

> ***Hebrews 3:1-6****: Therefore, holy brothers, who share in the heavenly calling, fix your thoughts on Jesus, the apostle and high priest whom we confess. He was faithful to the one who appointed him, just as Moses was faithful in all God's house. Jesus has been found worthy of greater honor than Moses, just as the builder of a house has greater honor than the house itself. For every house is built by someone, but God is the builder of everything. Moses was faithful as a servant in all God's house, testifying to what would be said in the future. But Christ is faithful as a son over God's house. And we are his house, if we hold on to our courage and the hope of which we boast.*

God's peace and abundant blessings to you all!

Your brother in Christ

George Denn

P.S: As an afterthought to this story, this miracle happened to me this afternoon. Ethan, the young man that has been working for me for a year and a half now, had pretty much made up his mind to go and work for his uncle next year. This news had saddened me. Like I said before, the guys that work here have always been more than just workers to me! Somehow I end up getting attached to every one of them and they become like sons to me! Ethan was no different, and last fall when I found out Ethan was intending to leave, I don't think if you'd have stuck a knife in me it could've hurt any worse. We had just stopped communicating and I just didn't know how to talk to him anymore. So I thought I would pray about it and as time went on, I just sort of accepted that Ethan wouldn't be here when springtime came around. However, about ten days ago Ethan called me and said he had been pondering something for a while now, and wanted to talk to me. I told him I would be back today. He came over around 1:00 this afternoon, telling me that he wanted to work for me again this year instead of for his uncle. But he also said that the job for his uncle still was in place if I didn't want him to come back. I told Ethan he had a job here. I also gave him a big hug and told him that I loved him. So there you go! Don't ever underestimate the power of prayer! It can move mountains and people, also! God never messes with your free will, but he will toy with your circumstances! I later found out that the other job would've paid $11 an hour, but Ethan wanted to work for me instead, even if I paid quite a bit less! I know that God is at work in this young man's life, but I still told him that maybe he needs his head examined!

HEY BY GEORGE! March 21, 2008

1 Corinthians -12:12-26: The body is a unit, though it is made up of many parts; and though all its parts are many, they form one body. So it is with Christ. For we were all baptized by one spirit into one body -whether Jews or Greeks, slave or free - and we were all given the one Spirit to drink. Now the body is not made up of one part, but many. If the foot should say, "Because I am not a hand, I do not belong to the body," it would not for that reason cease to be part of the body. And if the ear should say, "Because I am not an eye, I do not belong to the body," it would not for that reason cease to be part of the body. If the whole body were an eye, where would the sense of hearing be? If the whole body were an ear, where would the sense of smell be? But in fact God has arranged the parts in the body, every one of them, just as he wanted them to be. If they were all one part, where would the body be? As it is, there are many parts, but one body. The eye cannot say to the hand "I don't need you!" And the head cannot say to the feet "I don't need you!" On the contrary, those parts of the body that seem to be weaker are indispensable, and the parts that we think are less honorable we treat with special modesty, while our presentable parts need no special treatment. But God has combined the members of the body and has given greater honor to the parts that lacked it, so that there should be no division in the body, but that its parts should have equal concern for each other. If one part suffers, every part suffers with it; if one part is honored, every part rejoices with it.

On Wednesday I was supposed to take 50 bales of straw to a job site over by Eagle Lake, MN. The person that wanted the straw was using them for erosion control around some houses he is building over there. Ethan and I loaded it the night before down at Brad Scholl's place. The straw was payment for some fire wood that Brad had gotten from me earlier in the winter. We had the load all strapped down, and ready for me to take the next morning. So first thing Wednesday morning, cup of coffee in hand, I climbed aboard my red 1987 Ford pickup and headed down my driveway. But as I pulled out on the county road in front of my place and tried to put the transmission in the next gear, my clutch pedal just went to the floor. There was nothing there! I remember thinking, "I just hate mornings that start this way!" So in second gear, I maneuvered my load of straw onto a field driveway behind my brother's house and shut off the engine. I would have to wait until Ethan got home from school that afternoon so we could tow it to Blase's Car-X shop in town to get fixed. So I walked back home and got my Dodge Dakota. I had to reload the straw and make two trips instead of one, all the time wondering what the cost for the repair on the other pickup would be. Just like most other people, about the last thing I needed right then was a big repair bill, because I was thinking it would be around $500!

Earlier in the week, my seasonal depression was really acting up. It seems to get that way when winter doesn't go away when I think it should! For a couple of days there, I was feeling like one of the world's biggest losers. On Monday I had my friend, Jeff, stop in and pray for me. I felt better almost instantly, and I also felt that for all our Lord and Savior did for us, we are certainly not losers in his sight, so I needed to repent from this way of thinking!

2 Peter 1:3-11: His divine power has given us everything we need for life and godliness through our knowledge of him who called us by his own glory and goodness. Through these he has given us his very great and precious promises, so that through them you may participate in the divine nature and escape the corruption in the world caused by evil desires. For this very reason, make every effort to add to your faith goodness; and to goodness, knowledge; and to knowledge, self-control; and to self-control, perseverance; and to perse-verance, godliness; and to godliness, brotherly kindness; and to brotherly kindness, love. For if you possess these qualities in increasing measure, they will keep you from being ineffective and unproductive in your knowledge of our Lord Jesus Christ. But if anyone does not have them, he is nearsighted and blind, and has forgotten that he has been cleansed from his past sins. Therefore, my brothers, be all the more eager to make your calling and election sure. For if you do these things, you will never fall, and you will receive a rich welcome into the eternal kingdom of our Lord and Savior Jesus Christ.

So I have to ask myself who could want more than that?

This time of year there still isn't much going on, and our weather here in southern Minnesota hasn't quite made up its mind yet whether it wants to be spring or winter! Yesterday I drove to the post office to get my mail. I have to do this twice a week for a while because a guy by the name of Ken Schmit turned around suddenly in my driveway and hit my mailbox, busting off the post level with the ground. So until the frost goes out of the ground so that I can fix the mail box, I will pick up my mail in town twice a week! I saw God's sense of humor in all of this, because that morning I was praying for some provision, and Ken gave me $200 cash to fix my mail box! I told Ken that paying me for the mailbox wasn't necessary - accidents do happen, but he insisted so I took the money. Ken also asked for prayers for his brother, because he had just found out that his brother had a heart attack. He was talking on his cell phone when he swung around and ran over my mail box! So I told Ken I would pray for his brother, which I did. On my way to get my mail, the guy on the radio was talking about Mel Gibson's movie "The Passion of the Christ". Mel had been asked why he made the movie so graphic and the beatings so horrible. His answer was something to the effect that he had it made that way so that people wouldn't forget what Jesus actually went through for mankind. I agree with that, because sometimes I think we do forget what the Son of Man went through! Isaiah 52:14 tells just how badly he was beaten.

Just as there were many who were appalled at him- his appearance was so disfigured beyond that of any man and his form marred beyond human likeness.

I can safely say in my life I have never seen a man, nor animal, beaten beyond its likeness. So I decided I would watch the movie again, because, yes, we do forget sometimes what Jesus Christ went through for mankind, for you, for me! Sometimes we forget also that this Jesus we believe in did not stay dead! He is very much alive!

Matthew 28:2-7 There was a violent earthquake, for an angel of the Lord came down from heaven and, going to the tomb, rolled back the stone and sat on it. His appearance was like lightning, and his clothes were white as snow. The guards were so afraid of him that they shook and became like dead men. The angel said to the women," Do not be afraid, for I know that you are looking for Jesus, who was crucified. He is not here; he has risen, just as he said. Come and see the place where he lay. Then go quickly and tell his disciples: 'He has risen from the dead and is going ahead of you into Galilee. There you will see him.' Now I have told you".

Yes, seeing Mel's movie does reinforce all of this in my mind, but how quickly we can forget! This morning Terry and I were hauling a load of firewood to a guy about seven miles from here. On our way, a lady had slid into the ditch, as the road was covered with snow. I drove right passed her; I didn't even intend to stop. But Terry said we should've stopped and helped the lady out! So eventually, I did turn around and we stopped to help her. Another person stopped, as well, and after a few tries we managed to get her back up onto the road! A short time later my front end started to slide into a ditch. I was very close to being in the same predicament. So I was thankful we had turned around to help the lady out!

Proverbs 16:9: In his heart a man plans his course but the Lord determines his steps.

Just before Ethan and I went to deliver another load of firewood this afternoon, Blase called me and told me my truck was fixed. I asked him what the bill would be. He said $65. I was pretty shocked that it was so cheap! When I went to pick it up, Jeff, one of the guys that work for Blase, showed me this little plastic part that held another part that worked the clutch cylinder had broken and that was all that was wrong! This piece is not 1/2 inch by 1/2 inch, circular in design, and inside it has a hole big enough to slide a pen through. But if it's not in good condition, it has the power to bring a 3/4 ton pickup truck to a completely useless state! That's how important this $2 part is!

So how important is our part in the body of Christ?

1 Corinthians 12:27: Now you are the body of Christ, and each one of you is part of it.

I would have to say probably a pretty important part!

As I finish this story on Good Friday evening, I do want to recall what Jesus went through for mankind, for it is important that we never forget that. But something equally important that we must never forget is that He has risen, He has risen indeed!

God's peace and abundant blessings to you all!

Your brother in Christ,

George Denn

HEY BY GEORGE! April 7- 17, 2008

1 Corinthians 1:18-25: For the message of the cross is foolishness to those who are perishing, but to us who are being saved, it is the power of God. For it is written: "I will destroy the wisdom of the wise; the intelligence of the intelligent I will frustrate." Where is the wise man? Where is the scholar? Where is the philosopher of this age? Has not God made foolish the wisdom of the world? For since in the wisdom of God the world through its wisdom did not know him, God was pleased through the foolishness of what was preached to save those who believe. Jews demand miraculous signs and Greeks look for wisdom, but we preach Christ: a stumbling block to Jews and foolishness to Gentiles, but to those whom God has called, both Jews and Greeks, Christ, the power of God and the wisdom of God. For the foolishness of God is wiser than man's wisdom, and the weakness of God is stronger than man's strength.

Last Friday I finally did it! I finally sawed the old ash tree down that stood on the west side of my house. I had been putting it off for the last couple of years, but the rotten spot at the base of the trunk keep getting bigger and bigger. If I didn't take it down there was a good chance it would fall on my house. The day before I sawed it down, I had read an e-mail from Jeff's Uncle Pete telling of how a neighbor's tree had fallen and caused damage to his roof. To prevent this from happening again, he had four other trees taken down as well! One reason I was having such a hard time sawing it down was that it was the last tree in my farmyard that was here before I was! For practically 46 years this tree had been part of my life, and now I had to be the one to saw it down. We hooked several log chains to it and pulled on it with the skid loader so it would fall away from the house. I sawed with the chain saw, Ethan pulled with the skid loader and over it went - exactly where it was supposed to fall. "So much for 130 years of life", I thought when I had finished cutting it down! It was sort of like losing an old friend, and my yard sure looks bare and funny without it!

Ethan told me he would cut it up, because I had told Wayne Schwartz I would be at his place at ten o'clock. Wayne wanted to discuss some seed plans we had been talking about. So after I sawed down my old friend, the tree, I went to Wayne's. Wayne set out two chairs in his shop doorway and we sat down. Since neither one of us had too much of a plan, we decided we should pray first and ask the Lord to guide us.

Proverbs 21:30: There is no wisdom no insight, no plan that can succeed against the Lord.

Wayne told me that he always struggles with praying for the answers to situations. After all, didn't God give us a mind to think for ourselves? "He did," I told Wayne, "but there is a difference between looking to God for wisdom and following the wisdom of mankind!" My dilemma this spring, if in fact it even is a dilemma, is that I have 92 acres of certified organic land that I have to seed to hay sometime this year. I have pretty much decided that if I can't get it seeded this spring, I would do it later this summer when I had the funds to do it with. However, if I could get it seeded this spring, I probably would get some kind of crop of hay this fall and Wayne wouldn't have to locate another source. Also, if I could get it seeded this spring when I sow the oats and barley, I wouldn't have the additional cost of going over the ground again next summer. The only problem is that organic seed is about twice the cost of non-organic seed. So that leaves me with a need of $5400 to purchase the seed that I need on that land. We talked about several solutions but nothing definite was arranged.

Before I left, Wayne told me that he needed a "two fish and five loaves" type of miracle with his hay situation shortly, because his hay supply was starting to run low. He told me that he knew how many bales of hay he had left, and how long it would be before he would have pasture for his cows, and he knew he just wasn't going to have enough hay! I had been in this same situation several times myself. It isn't much fun so I knew what Wayne was going through, but that was before I learned to ask the Lord for help! So we did pray, and I asked the Lord for his abundance and not his scarcity in our situations. Wayne said he was a believer, and knew that God would do something! Just what that was, though, was hard to say. I have seen hay and grain last far longer than they should have, and one time I had some folks pray for me because I felt I was going to be short on some soybeans I had contracted, but when the bin was emptied, there were 800 more bushels in it than were supposed to be there! I also know that God doesn't always work in the same way every time, so we just had to wait and see what God would do!

That evening Wayne called me and said, "You'll never guess what happened!" He said he was getting a bale of hay from the top of the stack and was being very careful not to tip the stack over because it was the last row of bales. But to his amazement there was another row of bales behind that one! He told me that wasn't possible, because he had counted all the bales he had left seven to ten days ago. He had counted fourteen 3'x3'x8' large square bales, and had recounted them again to be sure. Yet on Friday afternoon when he counted them again, he had nineteen bales left - enough to see him through until he had pasture! I told Wayne that he had just witnessed a miracle, and that God surely had answered that prayer fast! The definition of a miracle is "a wonderful happening that is contrary to or independent of the known laws of nature"! I believe, too, that God has a plan for my situation as well! So let's just wait and see what it is.

> ***Ecclesiastes 8:4-7:*** *Since a king's word is supreme, who can say to him," What are you doing?" Whoever obeys his command will come to no harm, and the wise heart will know the proper time and procedure. For there is a proper time and procedure for every matter, though a man's misery weighs heavily upon him. Since no man knows the future, who can tell him what is to come?*

It is now April 17 and I can finish this story! After trying for nearly a week to find an avenue to buy my organic alfalfa seed, I finally decided that I was just going to have to wait until next summer to plant it and that was that. Or so I thought! It has been snowing here this year clear up to the 13 of April, so when my friend, Troy, called from Spring Valley and asked if I wanted to make a quick trip to Georgia, I jumped at the chance! I figured there wouldn't be any field work done around here for a while, anyway. So on Sunday morning around 11:00 a.m. we left Spring Valley, Minnesota for Dalton, Georgia. Troy was going down there to pick up some carpets from the factory that his brother-in-law, Tony, manages. While Troy was putting fuel in his diesel pickup I thought I smelled antifreeze. I almost mentioned it, but I figured Troy must smell it too, and that it probably wasn't anything important. One and a half hours into our trip we found out what the antifreeze smell was! Troy's water pump went out just a mile north of Urbana, Iowa. Troy called for a tow truck and he took us to Independence, Iowa, 17 miles north of where we broke down. Since this was Sunday, we couldn't get it fixed until the next day, so we would have to wait somewhere! Troy called his brother, Trent, who lived an hour straight east of there in Galena, Illinois. (I found out later that Galena is where Ulysses S. Grant was from!)

Trent and his friend, PJ, came to pick us up in PJ's Jeep. We learned on the way back that PJ worked on the same ship that found the Titanic, the Knorr, and the Atlantis. I had a feeling that this was going to be no ordinary adventure! Trent showed us where he lived and made arrangements for supper with some friends of his, Leslie and Sue. Leslie told us that the room where we were eating had previously been a garage, but one day when she came home, her gas pedal stuck and she drove her car right through the garage! So she just decided to make her house a little bigger instead of fixing the garage. Leslie's business card says "Rich Widow", and she has aspirations for running for mayor next year! Her friend, Sue, works at a place called Poopsies, and she makes birds out of dipper gourds! Sue says she buys her dried gourds for between $10-12 and sells the birds that she makes for as much as $700. Next, after supper and a movie, Trent arranged for us to stay at a house that another friend had built and was trying to sell. Before we went inside, all three of us noticed the moon was very bright in its half moon stage and we saw what looked like a white ring perfectly circling the moon. It was directly over us and we all commented that we had never seen that strange sight before! Inside the place, Trent showed us around.

I took the master bedroom with the king size bed and attached bathroom with a Jacuzzi tub. The house also had two big screen TV sets, one on each floor. I had to ask Trent what this house was worth. "$350,000" he said. That night while I lay in that big bed and the next morning while I was sitting in the Jacuzzi, I thought that this place was just too fancy for a guy like me! We never met the owner and it never cost us a cent to stay there. Like I always say, it's not what you know, but who you know that takes you places!

After we left the house, we went to a small shop in the main part of town, where a guy by the name of Bill roasts coffee beans and serves coffee daily to his friends, who range from retired brick layers to a federal agent to a mortician! The talk ranges from almost all topics local, state, national and world! My old neighbor, George, would have loved this group of people if he was still around! While I was there, I got the idea that Bill's coffee roasting machine would make a great pumpkin seed roasting machine also! Bill told me that I could find them for sale on the Internet so I will have to check it out sometime. After we left the coffee shop, we just walked around some. Troy was looking for a certain kind of tea, but the owner of the shop said the type he wanted was a something he was having trouble getting. Trent showed me a block-like thing that actually was tea, and these blocks of tea were used just like you would money. How times have changed! We stopped by Sue's shop and she showed us the birds that she made out of gourds. She said that she would send me some seeds from the gourds, and she might buy gourds from me in the future. We also went into a store that makes and sells all kinds of jams and salsas. I noticed a jar of pumpkin butter, so I had a taste - delicious! I thought I could probably market something like that in the fall with the other things I sell at my pumpkin stands.

Before I knew it, Trent was leading me upstairs to talk to Ivo, the owner of the store, so I asked him about his wholesale prices! After a hamburger lunch at a place called Georgio's, Trent took us past Grant's home. Trent was somewhat embarrassed about his junker car that he was driving us around in. I told Trent that I was way more at home in his car than in the house we stayed at the night before! Then our stay at this unique town was over. As Trent drove us back to Troy's pickup, I couldn't help but feel I had just spent the past day in the "twilight zone"! We said so long to Trent and waited for the pickup to be finished.

We finally left Independence at 5:00 p.m. and drove all that night and arrived at our destination in Dalton, Georgia at 8:00 a.m. Troy's brother-in-law, Tony, showed me the process for making carpets while Troy went about doing his business. All I can say is most people have no idea what goes into making carpets! As I watched Tony work with the complicated machines and the warp, it all reminded me of how God works in all of our lives and weaves them into a tapestry! Troy's other brother-in-law, Mike, drove us around town to the places where Troy needed to go. After dinner Mike left us, and we eventually ended up at Troy's father-in-law's home, where we spent the night and had breakfast. At 8:00 a.m. the next morning we left again for Minnesota - 978 miles according to Mike. This trip was just what I needed.

After breakfast back at Troy's place, we went to his shop in Spring Valley. Troy was selling me his generator, but I don't have to pay him until I get some money. We prayed for each other and parted ways. I came home, and this afternoon was able to get the seed that I needed! I was able to purchase it for half the regular price it would've cost me, and the guy I bought it from is carrying me until I get some money, at no interest until after August 1st! After supper I was able to get my first field worked for the season. Another year has begun! As I sit here tonight finishing up this story, I think of the fuel I'm going to need and the rent I have to pay yet this spring, and I wonder where it is all going to come from. I guess I am going to need another miracle!

> **Psalm 27:13-14:** *I am still confident of this: I will see the goodness of the Lord in the land of the living. Wait for the Lord; be strong and take heart and wait for the Lord.*

God's peace and abundant blessings to you all!

Your brother in Christ,

George Denn

HEY BY GEORGE! April 29, 2008

Ecclesiastes 7:8: The end of a matter is better than its beginning, and patience is better than pride.

Yesterday, Wayne Shwartz came by and hauled my old gray pickup to the scrap yard. Hardly any of it was gray anymore! It had two blue doors, a white box and a red tailgate. For the past couple years, we just referred to it as "THE HAMMER". Brad Claggett gave it that name. He said, "That truck is hammered beyond being hammered!" So the name just kind of stuck! It was unsafe for driving down the road any more, and for the past year it was banished to just driving around the farm here!

It was early to mid-June of 2004 when I got the truck. Brad was working on my farm then, and he and I had been praying for some time that spring for a pickup that I could use for a work truck. I had images in my head of something newer and bigger, but one day Paul Berry needed some hay and he mentioned he had this old Ford 4x4 pickup that he was trying to sell! So I traded him $1200 worth of hay for it! It was a gray 1980 1/2 ton Ford pickup - a far cry from what I thought God would give me. But I also knew that this was a gift from God and that I needed to be thankful for what he had provided, even if it wasn't what I had been expecting!

1 Thessalonians 5:8: Give thanks in all circumstances, for this is Gods will for you in Christ Jesus.

It would work to do the job I needed it to do. I had no money for anything better, so I was thankful, believe me! Brad even used it a few times to see his girlfriend Kelly! They were married last September. It pulled countless loads of hay and hauled countless loads of pumpkins, and made countless firewood deliveries. One time the first fall that I had it, the local news paper did a story about the pumpkins I sell. They took a picture of me and Charles Holladay unloading pumpkins off the old gray pickup. The next day it was on the front page of the Mankato Free Press, and somehow that picture ended up in a brochure that the Chamber of Commerce in this area puts out on local attractions!

The summer KY was here, he and Troy were hauling a load of hay with the pickup from a farm that I rent fourteen miles away. I had just sat down to eat some supper, when Troy called me. He told me that he and KY had wiped out on a corner pulling the load of hay! So trying to keep my cool, I went over to where they were at. Here was the old gray pickup parallel with and partly on the load of hay! I had to go and get a tractor so I could pull the truck off the load of hay! Troy had let KY drive and I guess the corner came up quicker than they thought. If I recall right, I think all I said to KY was "Do you remember last week when I was telling you not to try stopping too quickly with a load behind you? Well, this is why!" They were able to limp it home. The box had been dented somewhat, but now it was totally smashed!

That year was the year the tornado came through our area and a tree had fallen on my nephew, Mitch's, white pickup that he was storing here. The box was undamaged, so we took it off and put it on the old gray Ford, and once again it was as good as it ever was! We could never seem to get the signal lights to work right after that, though, so we just used it without them! That fall, Doug Johannsen was taking pictures while we were picking pumpkins and the old gray Ford found itself on the back cover picture of my first book! That fall, while Nate and I took KY back to his home in Wisconsin, Brad called and told me that he had dented the truck again on that same corner! Since then, I call that "wipeout corner"! Brad said that the old truck was just hammered! Since that time, we all just called it "THE HAMMER"!

Two other funny things happened that same fall that also involved THE HAMMER. One morning, Brad, KY, and myself were getting ready to pick pumpkins. KY wasn't quite ready, so he said he would meet Brad and me out in the field with THE HAMMER. Brad and I were picking pumpkins and we heard KY coming. He drove right by us and straight into a mud hole. He got stuck and then knocked the starter out at the same time! Keep in mind that KY was only 15 at the time and the field was very weedy. I've found that over the years I have not always explained things as well as I should have! I hope you can laugh at that experience now, KY, because now, so can I! I wouldn't trade that year you were here and the experiences we had for anything in the world!

We were picking the last load of pumpkins that year, as the harvest was finished. But a fight between Brad and Troy broke out! KY was in THE HAMMER, and I was starting to be upset with the way they were acting. So I told KY to back that truck up to where I was, and if those two didn't move, then run them over! So KY started to back up the pickup! I was totally ashamed of the conduct of all four of us that day. I led worship at church the next day and told the congregation that story, mentioning that it was one of the worst examples of Christianity I had ever seen! We should've been happy and excited for a job well done. I guess there was room for improvement in all four of us!

That winter Ron Porter was up here with Brad for two weeks in February. One day, Ron and I were down at brother Wayne's next door, sawing a tree. Not being from the north, Ron wasn't too good at driving in the snow! He got THE HAMMER stuck in some snow, locked up the front transfer case, and once again, the starter went out at the same time! Brother Wayne pulled it home for me, and there it sat until springtime. I just used it as a two-wheel drive ever since. It really was getting to be in bad shape, and I wouldn't let anyone drive it down the road, that is, except myself! That fall while we were hauling pumpkins, I would put a full load of pumpkins in front of me and a full load behind me. Quite often the cops would drive by this threesome and we would wave at them and they would wave at us, but we never once got pulled over! I figured if we did get pulled, over I would just pray and act dumb, which isn't too hard for me to do!

Ever since the fall of 2006, I have been blessed with something better to drive, so I had very little use for THE HAMMER anymore. Last summer Ethan put the blue doors on it from the blue pickup that he smashed! We did that because the passenger door wouldn't open, and the driver's side wouldn't close! We still used it last year to haul firewood and pumpkins, but only on the farm. Last fall when the work was all done, I filled it with firewood and parked it near the house, so it did still run the last time I used it! This spring, though, with scrap iron prices at $160 per ton and gas prices at $3.45 per gallon, I thought it was time to cash in THE HAMMER! Besides as Jesus said,

> **"Luke 12:15:** *Watch out! Be on your guard against all kinds of greed; a man's life does not consist in the abundance of his possessions."*

So the other day, I took off the white tailgate and replaced it with the red one that was shot on my red Ford. Then I took my skid loader and tipped THE HAMMER on its side, and with a bolt cutter, took off the gas tank and drained the oil from the motor, pulled it over to the shed and removed it's tires. Wayne Swartz came by yesterday afternoon, and we loaded it on his trailer. I received $305.60 for its iron! I just thought for all the experiences we had here on the farm with THE HAMMER, the least I could do was to give it a eulogy!

> **Ecclesiastes 12:13-14:** *Now all has been heard; here is the conclusion of the matter; fear God and keep his command-ments, for this is the whole duty of man. For God will bring every deed into judgment, including every hidden thing, whether it is good or evil.*

God's peace and abundant blessings to you all!

Your brother in Christ,

George Denn

HEY BY GEORGE! June 1, 2008

Luke 16:1-13: Jesus told his disciples: "There was a rich man whose manager was accused of wasting his posses-sions. So he called him in and asked him, 'What is this I hear about you? Give an account of your management, because you cannot be manager any longer.' The manager said to himself, ' What shall I do now? My master is taking away my job. I'm not strong enough to dig, and I'm ashamed to beg. I know what I'll do so that when I lose my job here, people will welcome me into their houses.' So he called in each one of his master's debtors. He asked the first, 'How much do you owe my master?' 'Eight hundred gallons of olive oil,' he replied. The manager told him, 'Take your bill, sit down quickly and make it four hundred.' Then he asked the second, 'And how much do you owe?' 'A thousand bushels of wheat,' he replied. He told him, 'Take your bill and make it eight hundred.' The master commended the dishonest manager because he had acted so shrewdly. For the people of this world are more shrewd in dealing with their own kind than are the people of the light. I tell you, use worldly wealth to gain friends for yourselves, so that when it is gone, you will be welcomed into eternal dwellings. Whoever can be trusted with very little can also be trusted with much. So if you have not been trustworthy in handling worldly wealth, who will trust you with true riches? And if you have not been trustworthy with someone else's property, who will give you property of your own? No servant can serve two masters. Either he will hate the one and love the other, or he will be devoted to the one and despise the other. You cannot serve both God and Money."

I was sitting in church today, and Pastor Dave Laack was using the scripture above - the parable of the shrewd manager. He asked us all the question, "How were we managing all that God had given us?" As he talked, I was thinking of an incident that had happened just lately with my hired man, Ethan. You see, Ethan isn't just my hired man, he is my friend, and I will always believe he was a gift from God sent here to help me. But that is never just a one way deal. I also believe that Ethan was sent here just like all the others so that he may learn something from me that God wanted him to know about. So we'll just say it's all a work in progress! I asked Ethan if he minded if I wrote about this. He told me it was OK, because he didn't care what people might think about him. I reassured him that no one would think of him in any way other than the fine young man that he is! They may think a lot less of me though! Here is the story!

A couple weeks ago, Ethan and I were out picking up rocks on the organic farm that I rent from Doris Berger. I noticed a familiar round obstacle in his back pocket! Familiar, I say, because I've seen these round cans in my Grandpa Denn's overall pockets, my uncle Lowell's pants pockets, and for more than twenty years in my own pants pockets. My young friend, Ethan, had started chewing tobacco. At first I was sad and mad all at the same time! Sad, because Ethan had started that same filthy habit I had for more than twenty years, and I knew what it is liable to do to him if he continues on with it! Mad, because this ridiculous habit keeps targeting our young people. I figure it's a habit from Hell. I base this on my own personal experience with the stuff!

John 10:10 The thief comes only to steal and kill and destroy; I have come that they may have life, and have it to the full

So tobacco will steal, kill, and destroy you! That's exactly what it eventually does to most of those who use it long enough, contrary to what Jesus has to offer, which is life to the full! I heard a story once that a man asked a pastor if he would go to Hell for using tobacco. The pastor thought a bit and answered the man, "No, but it will make you smell like you've been there!" I knew I was going to have to talk to Ethan soon if I noticed that he didn't quit using it. I didn't want to just say nothing, because then it would look like I was condoning it. But I didn't want to lash out at Ethan and cause a confrontation and condemn him for it, either. I prayed that Ethan would just give it up, and it would all simply go away, and I wouldn't have to say anything! Of course, that didn't happen! I went to the Lord with this, because I needed wisdom from him about what to say. Also, it had to be in his timing, not mine. It needed to come from God. After all, he knows Ethan and loves him far more than anyone on this earth ever could! I just kept praying about it. I asked Bob and Jeff, two friends of mine, to pray about it, too. As I was praying about it, I thought of all the years I wasted my money, my health and my relationship with the Lord and others with this awful habit!

I started chewing tobacco when I was about thirteen years old, so I was four years younger than Ethan was! My Grandpa Denn chewed tobacco and so did my Uncle Lowell. I looked up to these two men in my life, and I worked with them a lot. They were farmers; they worked hard and they were tough, and I wanted to be like them. So I started to chew tobacco just like they did. I don't exactly recall the all the details anymore. I do remember my Mom crying about it all. Little did I care at the time how it broke her heart to see her son do this! After some time had passed, she would even buy it for me in town if I asked her to pick it up for me. I also remember my oldest brother, Wayne, whacking me upside the head because I had been arguing with Mom about it. He hit me so hard it broke my eardrum! It is ironic, but the doctor who fixed my ear, fixed it with a piece of cigarette paper! My brother, Wayne, smoked so he wasn't the greatest role model either. My mother asked my Grandpa Denn if he would talk to me about it. All he said was that it wasn't a very good thing for me to do, but that didn't carry a whole lot of weight, because he was telling me all that with a chew in his mouth! My uncle just laughed about it because that's just something men do. One positive statement my Dad said that I have never forgotten to this day was, "Sometimes it takes more of a man not to do something!" However, that didn't stop me from chewing. My dad told me that if I was going to chew, then I had to be man enough to buy it in the store myself. So I did; no one ever questioned how old I was!

I also smoked cigars and pipes, sometimes both at the same time. Remember, I was trying to be tough! But, alas, one can only abuse their body so much and after years of chewing a can of snuff a day, it started to take its toll! I started getting sores inside my mouth. I would move the chew around, but the sores would just spread!

My dentist, Bryan Johnson, said, "George, I don't want to be the one to tell you that you have mouth cancer! QUIT before it is too late! You already have the first signs of it, and it can kill you if you get it. Please quit!" I remember walking out of his office that day wondering, "How can this be? This can't happen to a tough guy like me!" But it *was* happening! Not only is it a blow to one's pride to find out that you're not as invincible as you thought, but then you realize that the stuff is killing you, and you are powerless to quit. It has that much of a hold on you! Well, I had to cry out to God Almighty to help me to quit. I had just recently started taking my calling with the Lord seriously and had started attending the church I belong to now. I was going to Rapid City, South Dakota in the fall of 1995 to a Christian gathering that was taking place out there. For ten days I would be around people who didn't use tobacco. So I asked the people I went with to pray about this for me. I threw the tobacco away and for ten days it didn't bother me a bit, not like the many times I'd tried to quit and failed. I felt protection from the Almighty! But when I got home, soybean harvest was in full swing. I was having a bad day, the combine broke down, and Dad and I got into an argument. I needed a chew! So I jumped into my pickup and took off for Madison Lake to buy a can of snuff! I remember asking God to help me, because if he didn't, I was going to start chewing again! "See, I'm even driving to get a can!"

> *1 Corinthians 10:13: No temptation has seized you except what is common to man. And God is faithful; he will not let you be tempted beyond what you can bear. But when you are tempted, he will also provide a way out so that you can stand up under it.*

I got to the market, and just before I could tell Mike "Give me a can of Copenhagen!" I noticed something on his counter. It said, "All mint chew"! I asked Mike, "What is that stuff?" He said It was some new product that a salesman had just dropped off just a little while ago. He read the ingredients; they said, "Ground mint leaves, a safe alternative to tobacco". "Give me a can of that," I said. I showed it to Bryan, my dentist. He read the can and told me that there wasn't a thing in that stuff that could hurt you. He even asked me where I got it from and was going to recommend it to some of his other patients who chewed! I ended up chewing this stuff for about two more years. It really helped me get over the nicotine addiction. However, I still had that physical addiction to chewing. My nephews were always around me, and were getting to be the same age that I was when I started chewing. I didn't want to be the same bad influence my Grandpa and uncle were on me. So I gave it up. I quit on a Monday and was going to Hot Springs, Arkansas on Saturday. I would be gone for about ten days again. The day before I was to leave, I was trying to get some road ditch hay put up. My Dad was over that day trying to help me, but he seemed to be doing everything wrong. And of course, here came the big black rain cloud! I went over to where my dad was and just let him have it with my tongue! I walked back to my pickup since it had just started to rain. My friend, Terry, was in the pickup, as he had been out helping me that day. When I opened the door and sat down, he said laughing, "I bet a chew would taste real good right about now!" I said, "It would, but I'm not going to!" He said "You need to apologize to your Dad, too, before you leave." I said, "I know, and I'll do it shortly." Dad would be back to his place in about an hour.

That all happened twelve to fourteen years ago. I haven't had anything to chew since then and I want to keep it that way! So it is real hard for me to see young people I care about heading down the same road that I was on, after all I went through with my tobacco experience! The right time did come on Friday evening after the work was done. I was able to talk to Ethan about it without either one of us getting mad. I mentioned that this was a Christian business and I didn't feel that chewing tobacco glorified God very much. Besides, I didn't need the temptation around me, either; and that if he did use it while he was working for me, that he would be doing it against my wishes! I also told Ethan that it hurt me to see him start this habit because I cared about him, and I know firsthand what it can do to you. I also told Ethan that I was praying for him that he would stop before it became too big of a habit. I guess the rest is between Ethan and the Lord.

Proverbs 24:11-12: *Rescue those being lead away to death; hold back those staggering towards slaughter. If you say, "But we knew nothing about this," does not he who weighs the heart perceive it? Does not he who guards your life know it? Will he not repay each person for what he has done?*

God's peace and abundant blessings to you all!

Your brother in Christ,

George Denn

Added on 8/12/2008: A few weeks after the above story was written, I was spraying pumpkins. Ethan was doing some mowing on another field that I rent. The motor for my sprayer broke, so I needed to buy a new one. I had to go into town, but first, I went over to where Ethan was working to see how he was doing. I noticed that Ethan had a chew of tobacco in his mouth. I didn't say anything at the time, but it really did make me angry that he was doing this when I had asked him not to while working for me or around me. In anger, I wrote Ethan a note and put it in his pickup so he'd see it when he went home, But a short time later, I ripped up the note because what I'd said was out of anger! So I had to ask Jesus what to write. This is what I wrote in the note: "Just a friendly reminder, Ethan, that this is a tobacco-free farm. I hope that wasn't tobacco I saw you chewing today! Your friend, George." I put it in his pickup and never said another word. That Sunday, Ethan stopped in for a couple hours. Before we started to work Ethan said," I have a confession to make. I was chewing tobacco on Friday. I was bored out there and I fell into temptation." I told Ethan that I knew all about temptation and that I've succumbed to it many times myself, and that he was forgiven! I asked Ethan to see it from my perspective, too. "If you don't respect me on this issue, do you respect me on any?" I went on to say that integrity is what a person does when no one else is around! So, hopefully, we have resolved the tobacco issue - at least around here!

HEY BY GEORGE!   **July 14, 2008**

Revelation 14:14-16: I looked, and there before me was a white cloud, and seated on the cloud was one "like a son of man" with a crown of gold on his head and a sharp sickle in his hand. Then another angel came out of the temple and called in a loud voice to him who was sitting on the cloud, "Take your sickle and reap, because the time to reap has come, for the harvest of the earth is ripe." So he who was seated on the cloud swung his sickle over the earth, and the earth was harvested.

A week ago we pulled the old grain binder out of the shed. Last Thursday and Friday, Ethan and I made a new canvas that elevates the cut stalks of grain to the tying mechanism, and then we greased it up. I had decided that on Monday (that is today) we would cut the wheat. Every year I do this to sell the bundles with the pumpkins in the fall. We put the three canvases on the binder, I climbed onto the binder seat, and Ethan drove the tractor. Then we began to cut the wheat. The start of the harvest had begun! The wheat was still a little green, though, but these bundles will only be used for show so I could cut it a little earlier than I normally would! I had to get these cut, because it was the last major thing I needed to get done before I went off for two weeks to the two Christian youth camps that I serve at: Northern Lights and Heartland SEP.

Each year before I use this antique piece of machinery I always say a prayer, because it can be a real contraption to run! Canvases can slip, bundles can mis-tie, and I almost went flying off the seat twice when the bull wheel hit a bump in the field! I was holding onto one of the leavers, so I managed to stay on the seat. Today we seemed to have had our share of problems with this cantankerous machine! Ethan asked me if I had prayed before we started. I told him I had, and just to think how bad it would've been if I hadn't prayed! One by one, we solved the problems that arose and after six hours, we had a couple of acres of wheat bundled.

Galatians 6:7-9: Do not be deceived: God cannot be mocked. A man reaps what he sows. The one who sows to please his sinful nature, from that nature will reap destruction; the one who sows to please the Spirit, from the Spirit will reap eternal life. Let us not become weary in doing good, for at the proper time we will reap a harvest if we do not give up.

Well, we didn't give up, but we were pretty glad when the last bundle went through the machine, and I know a lot of people will enjoy these bundles this fall when they decorate.

While I was riding on the seat of this unique machine, I watched as the cut wheat stalks fell back on the canvas platform, were elevated up to the tying mechanism, and then fell as bundles to the ground after they were tied. The machine makes a mixture of sounds, if you can imagine the "snick, snick, snick" from the sickle; the continuous zinging sound from the chains, and the "click, click, click" sound from the knotter as each bundle was made - not to mention the sound of the tractor plus some noises coming from places that tell me I am fortunate that this machine runs at all! While I was hearing this and watching all the goings-on, some thoughts rolled through my head! Eighty-six days ago I planted this field to wheat, and that is what I was harvesting today. The seed came from wheat that I had harvested a year ago. I had it cleaned and bagged, and stored it in my granary all winter. On my birthday, April 20th, I opened up the wheat sacks and filled my grain drill. My friend, Jeff, and I prayed over the seed, asking that it would glorify God and be used for his kingdom purposes.

Psalm 37:5-6: Commit your way to the Lord; trust in Him and he will do this: He will make your righteousness shine like the dawn, the justice of your cause like the noonday sun.

While I was listening to this great orchestra play (compliments of the McCormick-Deering company, the forerunner of International Harvester), I was thinking that it was far too early to be harvesting this wheat. The bundles will look nice as decorations when they dry down, but the grain will be shrunken and light! If I wait until the grain is ripe, the bundles will not be as nice looking for decorating, but the grain will be hard and good for flour or seed. My former pastor, Charles, once asked me how I knew when a crop was ripe to harvest. I asked him how he knew what kind of sermon to preach. You just know he said. I told him it was the same way with harvesting a crop - you just know when it is ready!

This evening as I am writing, this I am very tired and am thinking of the lyrics of a funeral song they were singing in a show I watched last night.

> I'm kind of homesick for a country
> To which I've never been before;
> No sad goodbyes will there be spoken,
> For time won't matter anymore.
> *Refrain:* Beulah land, I am longing for you,
> And someday on thee I'll stand;
> Where my home shall be eternal
> Beulah land, sweet Beulah land.

Some day you will find me there instead of here, but if that doesn't happen tonight, tomorrow you will find Ethan and me shocking wheat in a field on the farm where God has placed me, on the northwest side of Wita Lake, today we used the Mcormick-Deering to harvest, but I will definitely be ready when the "International Harvester" comes!

God's peace and abundant blessings to you all!

Your brother in Christ

George Denn

HEY BY GEORGE!   July 29, 2008

1 Timothy 1:12-17 I thank Jesus our Lord, who has given me strength, that he considered me faithful, appointing me to his service. Even though I was once a blasphemer and a persecutor and a violent man, I was shown mercy because I acted in ignorance and unbelief. The grace of our Lord was poured out on me abundantly, along with the faith and love that are in Christ Jesus. Here is a trustworthy saying that deserves full acceptance: Christ Jesus came into the world to save sinners - of whom I am the worst. But for that very reason I was shown mercy so that in me, the worst of sinners, Christ Jesus might display his unlimited patience as an example for those who would believe on him and receive eternal life. Now to the King eternal, immortal, invisible, the only God, be honor and glory for ever and ever. Amen.

As I start to write this story, I am sitting in the white gazebo at Camp Eagle Crest about twenty miles north of Peoria, Illinois. For the last ten days I have been away from home and enjoying summer camp life. Besides, Ethan is back there taking care of things so I'm sure there is nothing to worry about! My first week was spent in southeastern MN at Eagle Bluff Education Center where the summer camp "Northern Lights" is sponsored by the Worldwide Church of God, the church that I am a member of. And now I'm here at Heartland S.E.P., which is sponsored by the same church. To me, this all feels like more of a vacation than anything! I haven't seen most of my friends down here for about a year. Of course, I've been telling a few stories from back home.

One story took place while I was replanting squash after Striped Gophers had eaten most of the first planting. I asked God that morning if he would show himself in a big way, because I was wondering where he was in all of this! Paul Schwartz and I were planting squash later that day. At one point, I traded places with Paul to ride the planter for a while. As I climbed onto the planter seat with my three-gallon pail of squash seeds, I noticed a single seed lying on the platform. I picked up the seed to plant it and I noticed a perfect cross imbedded on the seed. I wondered, "What are the chances of that one seed out of the thousands in the pail to be lying right there where I could see it?"

Another day I wanted to spray twenty-two acres of millet for broadleaf weeds. The problem was that the fuel gauge on my tractor showed empty and I only had $65 left. I also needed to buy some groceries. At $4.65 per gallon for diesel fuel, I could either buy fuel or buy groceries, but I couldn't do both. So I asked God to help stretch the fuel. I got my spraying done and went to town that evening and bought groceries!

Hebrews 4:14-16: Therefore since we have a great high priest who has gone through the heavens, Jesus the son of God, let us hold firmly to the faith we profess. For we do not have a high priest who is unable to sympathize with our weaknesses, but we have one who has been tempted in every way, just as we are- yet was without sin. Let us then approach the throne of grace with confidence, so that we may receive mercy and find grace to help us in our time of need.

This year at Northern Lights Camp, I was counselor for the boys' dorm Group 4, ages ten through fourteen. In my dorm were: James, Hunter, Liam, David, Austin, Zachery, and Caleb. Dan Jensen was our chaperone and Ted Gamble was our co- counselor. Doug, Troy and Ian would also join us at dorm chat time. This took some of the pressure off me to come up with stuff to talk about! This year the messages at both camps were based on Timothy. You can read about him and the letters that the Apostle Paul wrote to him in 1st and 2nd Timothy in your Bible. Timothy had a Greek father and a Jewish mother, and was pulled in two different directions as he grew up! The Greeks worshipped a god by the name of Zeus, an old man type figure with full flowing beard, just ready to send down lightning bolts if you did something wrong! But the Jewish people worshiped the God of Abraham, Isaac, and Jacob - the same God I worship - the Triune God, the one that is *for* you, and not against you! Timothy was very young, probably between fifteen and eighteen when he decided to throw his allegiance in full to his mother's God. The apostle Paul was his mentor and what a great job he did! How many of us can convince young men of that age that Jesus Christ is real? The reason was that Jesus Christ was very real in Paul's life and Timothy saw all of this!

My dorm boys participated in fishing, with Caleb catching the most fish, putting our dorm in the lead for that activity. Austin was a pro in archery and we gave him an award for the most bull's-eyes. One day our group took some pictures for the movie we were making, "Converted Cannibals or a Whole Bunch of Nonsense!" One of the boys accidentally ended up throwing Dan Jensen's underwater camera in the Root River and it flowed gently down the stream and sank! Our attempts to find it were futile and a collection was made so he could get a new one. The young man later apologized to Dan and we gave him an award for humility. On another day our group went river canoeing on a three and a half mile stretch on the Root River. Several times our canoe lost its course and it seemed like we just helplessly twirled down the river. Once I was able to grab on to a fallen tree branch and the current of the river straightened us out!

When Northern Lights ended, I felt spiritually full; that is the only way I can describe it! I always wanted to do two camps back to back, and this year I got my chance! After camp ended up in Minnesota, I drove six and a half hours to the Illinois camp, where I am now writing this. Bob Shippits and co-counselor, Derek, just walked by with Boys Dorm 4B and some friendly banter was exchanged. My responsibilities this year here are not so hectic or stressful, as I am only on security. Mostly we take staff where they need to go, and put water and Gatorade in strategic places for the campers while they do their activities. We also watch at night for any mischievous activities that may be taking place, but they are usually very rare! Yesterday, Teshome came up and shook my hand. The last time I saw him was at Snowblast winter camp a year and a half ago. He and I stayed up until 3:00 a.m. having a talk. Teshome mentioned he may go into the Air Force after camp, so the next camp he goes to might be boot camp! Excuse me for a while...I have to take Mary Camble and Janet Gartner down to the lodge in the "Gator".

I just got back, so I can finish writing about Ky, the young man that was at my place three years ago. I talked to his mom, Denise, and she told me that she'll be taking him to Green Bay College when she gets home. He plans to major in business. I told Denise to tell Ky "hi" from me and that I loved him! She also told me that he had raised some pumpkins this year. Hmmm, I wonder where he got that from? Just when I was wondering if my life had any meaning to it at all, God showed me these two boys and how he had used me to minister to them! Tomorrow, if it is in God's plan I will give the morning devotion for staff at breakfast time, so I guess that's all I have to write about for now.

James 4:13-17: Now listen, you who say, "Today or tomorrow we will go to this or to that city, spend a year there, carry on business and make money." Why, you do not even know what will happen tomorrow. What is your life? You are a mist that appears for a little while and then vanishes. Instead, you ought to say, "If it is the Lord's will, we will live and do this or that." As it is, you boast and brag; all such boasting is evil. Anyone, then, who knows the good he ought to do and doesn't do it, sins.

August 1

As we head towards the end of camp, looking back a few days, I always say that you can tell stories about camp, and then tell stories about what *really* went on at camp! Since I last wrote, we experienced a storm where the campers and staff had to go to the tornado shelters, which is good, as I was always wondering "Where we should go?" So far I have lived through three or four tornados and every time I needed a basement, there wasn't time to get to one! Later that evening we got to talk to the boys about courage and how it might look like if they had to exercise that trait one day?

Another day we were out on the paint ball course. Teshome was behind me and shot his gun at someone. I could feel the paint ball go across my hair! Teshome said he was sorry; I just told him I usually part my hair in the front of my head!

This morning I went to chapel and there was a nice recliner chair with a sign on it, saying, "THIS CHAIR IS RESERVED FOR

GEORGE DENN." Tracy Porter did this because I tend to nod off during worship! So everyone got a good laugh, including me! I always felt they should have recliner chairs at church!

Right now, I have a young man with me that they pulled from activities because his behavior was less than appropriate. So as I am watching him, he is also helping me. Later he will help Mike while I go to "staff versus camper paintball". While I was watching this young man, I kept thinking of this verse:

Matthew 25:40: *The King will reply, "I tell you the truth, whatever you did for one of the least of these brothers of mine, you did for me."*

It made me want to treat him with kindness, as that's the way I would like to be treated if it was me. Earlier in the week I had been walking past the swings, and I overheard a young girl from dorm 1G exclaim to one of her friends, "Those boys from 1B are just plain evil, most of them!" The statement made me laugh! After spending time with this young man from 1B, I would have to say that they probably just need working with a little! Well, I have to go again to get some girls from paint ball and then we'll have homemade pizza for lunch. See you later!

Camp ended on a positive note this year, with seven baptisms taking place after camp. Also, two were baptized earlier in the week, so there was a total of nine baptisms this year.

When it was time to leave camp, Tony had to jumpstart my pickup because the battery was dead. As I pulled into the Freedom gas station in Lacon, my truck died. I wondered what I was going to do. Here I was in the middle of nowhere, I had $140 on me, and my cell phone was dead. Oh, great! I asked a young man by the name of Dustin if he had a pair of jumper cables. He tried to get my truck going, but couldn't. I plugged my phone into Dustin's pickup, and was able to reach Linda back at camp. But of course, the reception is poor there, so she couldn't understand what I was saying very well! About that time, I saw Mark Lengwin, the life guard from camp, pull up to the stop sign! I waved Mark down and he pulled in to help. He told me he would take me to get a new battery, so I gave Dustin $20 and thanked him for helping me. Mark drove to Chillicothe, a small town about eight miles south on the other side of the river from Lacon. We stopped at an O'Riley's Auto Parts store where I bought a battery and a crescent wrench for $96. While we were in the store, one of the fellows there asked if we were down for the summer program. I said "Yes, but how would you know that?" He said he had attended summer camp for four years and Snowblast in Minnesota for two years. He had recognized us as soon as we'd walked through the door! I asked him his name about the same time that I noticed it on his shirt. His name is Josh and I have a picture of him right here. He was in Tom Burnett's and my dorm the first year we held Snowblast in 2003! As we left, I once again told Josh that it was good to see him. When Mark and I got into his van, we both agreed that things like this just don't happen for no reason! We drove back to Lacon and put the battery in and away I went! Many thanks, Mark, for all your help, and something tells me that I haven't seen the last of Josh, either.

2 Timothy 2:6-13: Remember Jesus Christ, raised from the dead, descended from David. This is my gospel, for which I am suffering even to the point of being chained like a criminal. But God's word is not chained. Therefore I endure everything for the sake of the elect, that they too may obtain the salvation that is in Christ Jesus, with eternal glory. Here is a trustworthy saying: If we died with him, we will also live with him; if we endure, we will also reign with him. If we disown him, he will also disown us; if we are faithless, he will remain faithful, for he cannot disown himself.

Like I always say, connections are everything!

God's peace and abundant blessings to you all!

Your brother in Christ,

George Denn

HEY BY GEORGE!   **August 23, 2008**

*Proverbs 1:7, 29:26: The fear of the Lord is the beginning
of knowledge, but fools despise wisdom and knowledge. He
who trusts in himself is a fool, but he who walks in wisdom
is safe.*

Wayne Schwartz had asked me to go along with him to The
Minnesota State Fair, or the "Great Minnesota Get Together", as it
has come to be called - that is, if I didn't have anything better to do
on Saturday. I haven't been there in ten years so I told Wayne that I
would go with him. His son, Paul, was showing a crossbred heifer
that day and Wayne was going up for that. We planned to leave at
8:30 a.m. this morning, but Wayne called me at 6:30 a.m., telling me
that his plans had changed and I should be at his place as close to
7:30 a.m. as I possibly could! Something should have told me right
there that this wasn't going to be your ordinary day, because Wayne
doesn't usually get up until 8:00 a.m! Well, I hurried up and got over
to Wayne's right at 7:30, and we took off for the fair. Before we left, I
asked Wayne if I should bring my cell phone. He thought that would
be OK just in case something happened! As we drove, I thought I
smelled alfalfa hay. Shortly after that thought, Wayne revealed to
me that he had a bale of hay in his trunk, because Paul asked him to
bring him some because he'd underestimated the amount he needed.
About fifteen minutes into our trip, Wayne's Saturn died on us; the
battery was dead! It was a good thing I had brought my phone! First,
Wayne asked me to pray for our situation. Then we called back to
his place and got a hold of his daughter, Catherine (which Wayne
said was a miracle in itself!) Wayne told her to wake up Peter and
have him call my phone. Peter called and Wayne told him where we
were, and said to get a battery out of his H Farmall tractor and bring
it to us. About this time, Paul called and mentioned that they were
going to start judging cows earlier than was planned! So much for
my frugal friend's theory about cell phones - in his own words, "I
can live without one." I just mentioned that there was nothing wrong
with being Amish, either!

One of the more amusing things I saw while we sat and waited for Peter to come with the battery was this: car after car was going to the Pioneer Power show. I bet 100 cars went by, but only one stopped and asked if we needed any help. I guess everyone was in a hurry to get back to a simpler time when neighbors helped one another out!

Ecclesiastes 7:10: Do not say, "Why were the old days better than these?" For it is not wise to ask such questions.

Well, Peter showed up with the battery and we were off! I bought breakfast at McDonald's; Wayne said it was the first time that he'd ever gone through a drive-through and the first time he'd had an Egg McMuffin! You have to remember here that Wayne is frugal. Shortly after this, Paul called and wanted to talk to his dad. Another first, Wayne was talking on a cell phone while he was driving! Will wonders ever cease?! About three miles south of our destination, Wayne said that we were about to have problems again with the car, and confessed that it was his fault because he had procrastinated in fixing the alternator! "Procrastination," someone once said, "is a thief of time." I know how Wayne was feeling, because I have the very same frailty! However, the Lord was watching over us. The car quit on a hill and we were able to coast to the bottom and there was a repair shop across the street from where we came to a stop! Now, my friend Wayne was about to be stretched again, because he generally does all his own repair work, and to have someone else do what he could do himself goes against all frugality! However, his son Paul was more important to him, so he would let others fix his car this time! One more thing I saw - Wayne picked up a twenty dollar bill laying on the ground, handed it to the attendant and told the man it wasn't his! You could tell by the man's expression that it wasn't his, either! I was thinking "I wish I could find some money right about now because here I am going to the State Fair, and I only have $4.50 on me and it costs $11.00 to get in! So if you're thinking my friend Wayne is a project, just remember this - it takes one to know one! I'm sorry, but that's all God would let me take. Does he not say in his word:

Philippians 4:19: *"And my God will meet all your needs according to his glorious riches in Christ Jesus."*

As a matter of fact, yesterday I had no fuel and no money to buy any to do my work, and as this day dawned, I was still in the same predicament. So I figured I might as well go to the fair while I was waiting for God to provide! Well, Wayne's car wouldn't be fixed until afternoon. This left us with a choice: call a cab or take the bus, since the bus stop was just across the street. We decided to take the bus. Since neither of us had ever ridden a city bus, we had no clue of times or cost. There was a women standing there, so we asked her if she was waiting for the bus, if she knew how long the wait would be, and if it would take us to the fair grounds. We found out that the bus would be there in about seven minutes and it probably would take us right to the fair. Earlier, I had called Paul and told him that the car clunked out and we may not make it in time. So now I called him back and told him there still might be a chance that we would make it, but we wouldn't be able to bring his bale of hay. It would have looked so ridiculous that even we didn't want to try it! Wayne asked the bus driver if the bus went to the fair. He told Wayne that it stopped right by the gate. So the bus ride wasn't too bad after all, and now we wouldn't have to pay the $8 per car parking charge, because Wayne had forgotten his free parking tickets back home. Wayne, knowing my financial status, paid for my way into the fair!

Well, we had arrived, and in short order we made it to the Coliseum before Paul showed his heifer. We even were able to talk to Paul before he went in! Paul's heifer took third place and was awarded a blue ribbon. After that Wayne and I just walked around some until it was time to leave. We went through the sheep and goat barns. I stopped rubbed this red goat in the head, thinking, "He sure looks like an ugly Gomer!" I told Wayne that this place reminded me about the story of the sheep and the goats.

Matthew 25:31-34: When the Son of Man comes in his glory, and all the angels with him, he will sit on his throne in heavenly glory. All the nations will be gathered before him, and he will separate the people one from another as a shepherd separates the sheep from the goats. He will put the sheep on his right and the goats on his left. Then the King will say to those on his right, "Come, you who are blessed by my Father; take your inheritance, the kingdom prepared for you since the creation of the world."

Wayne said that he always wondered about that scripture and its meaning. I said, "I think I would rather be a sheep than a goat!" After that, Wayne struck up a conversation with a guy who drove an ox cart from Pembina, North Dakota to the State Fair. He said he started out on July 1st and got there on the 20th of August! And we thought it took us a long time to get here! Well, at least he didn't have to buy gas, but his wheels looked like they could use some grease! Shortly after that Wayne bought us a milk shake and we went into the 4-H building. After our tour in there, it was about time for us to leave. On our way to the gate, a parade came down the street. Somebody had a couch that they had motorized, and was driving it down the street. It even had a license plate! Now that's my kind of vehicle! We had to ask for help again to find out how to get to the bus that would take us back. It turned out that we were on the wrong side of the street from where we needed to be. We no more than got across the street and the bus was there! I think I have a pretty good idea now how this bus riding works! Wayne told me that he was humbled by asking for all this help today! He also mentioned as people got off the bus, you would probably never see that person again. When we got to our street, we got off the bus. As we were walking across the street, the lady that had helped us earlier in the morning was crossing the street coming in our direction! She said, "I see you made it back!" After she passed us, I asked Wayne, "I wonder what the chances were of that happening in a city this big?"

Hebrews 13:2: Do not forget to entertain strangers, for by doing some have entertained angels without knowing it.

Wayne paid for the car repair and they gave him a free car wash, another first for Wayne today! He said he didn't think he had ever washed this car before! We still had the bale of hay in the trunk so we had to go back to the fair and give it to Paul. Paul and I kept in touch by cell phone until we found a spot between the cow barn and the Coliseum outside the fence. While others looked on, we got the bale of hay out of the trunk and waited for Paul to show up on his side of the fence. Wayne took one twine and I took another and at the count of three, we pitched the bale of hay over the fence. Our mission was complete, and you could tell Paul was happy to have the hay to feed his cow!

Some day at the end of time, there will be another great gathering far greater than the "Great Minnesota Get Together", and I am sure with the same amount of variety in the people!

Luke 13:29: People will come from east and west and north and south and take their places at the feast in the Kingdom of God.

You have a place at that feast! Jesus has paid the price. All you have to do is go!

Revelation 22:12-17: Behold, I am coming soon! My reward is with me, and I will give to everyone according to what he has done. I am the Alpha and the Omega, the First and the Last, the Beginning and the End. Blessed are those who wash their robes, that they may have the right to the tree of life and may go through the gates into the city. Outside are the dogs, those who practice magic arts, the sexually immoral, the murderers, the idolaters and everyone who loves and practices falsehood. I, Jesus, have sent my angel to give you this testimony for the churches. I am the Root and the Offspring of David, and the bright Morning Star. The Spirit and the Bride say, "Come!" And let him who hears say, "Come!" Whoever is thirsty, let him come; and whoever wishes, let him take the free gift of the water of life.

Now that's one "Get Together" you're not going to want to miss! See you there! But in the meantime, someone just paid me today after I got home from the fair, so it's time to cut some more hay!

God's peace and abundant blessings to you all!

Your brother in Christ,

George Denn

HEY BY GEORGE!   **November 14-15, 2008**

1 Corinthians 9:10: Surely he says this for us, doesn't he? Yes, this was written for us, because when the plowman plows and the thresher threshes, they ought to do so in the hope of sharing in the harvest.

I just didn't want to have to make this phone call! My family has rented this farm from Bob and his family for the past 47 years now. But the rent is due on the 15th of November, and if I don't come up with $8000 by tomorrow to pay the rent, I will have to call Bob and for the first time in 47 years, I will have to tell him I have no money for him! My pumpkin crop this year was worse than terrible! I do have enough hay on hand if it sells to pay my expenses and get me into next year. It seems, though, in these tough economic times people just are not buying until they absolutely need it. In my case it is hay. Well, I figure I have done everything within my power that I can do. I have grown it, baled it, and advertised it. God has to provide the buyers, for I cannot do my part and his part also!

This year was probably one of the toughest years that I've ever experienced here! Yet when I look back on it all, I can see miracle after miracle that has brought me to this point. With the price of fuel this year, most days it seemed like we were farming with an empty tank! A couple of times Ethan would ask me, "How will we do the work we have to do tomorrow?" All I could say was, "I don't know. It isn't tomorrow yet!" After a while I would say to Ethan, "I don't know what we will do for fuel tomorrow." Ethan would say, "Oh, something will come up; it always does!" Somehow we always had enough for the day at hand

This continued on until late August. Chris Shenk was buying some hay from me and he stopped out in the field where I was baling. He asked me how long before I needed some money, because his finances were also in the tank! I just laughed and said, "About two months ago!" I said this to Chris, knowing my tractor could run out of fuel at any moment! Really! "I don't care," I told Chris, "but fuel is my biggest Issue." Chris called the fuel company right away and had them bring out 600 gallons the next morning. I almost thought

I had died and gone to heaven, to have an abundance of fuel for the first time all year!

As we started picking pumpkins this fall, I could see that I wasn't going to have hardly any to sell. The year had been way too dry for vine crops. So I had to tell everyone that I had supplied in the past that I couldn't give them any this year. Instead of the four stands I usually run, I could only supply the one here at the farm. It was nice not having all that extra work to do, but I did miss the $40,000 that it had brought in last year!

With my work load fairly light this fall, I was able to take in my church's fall celebration down at Wisconsin Dells, which took place at the Kalahari. Ethan, Dylan, Paul and Terry took care of things for the four days I was gone. I hadn't really planned on going because of my finances, but I was urged by several people, telling me I really needed to go. I called my friend, Troy, and told him if he could get me a room at such a late date that I would go! He not only took care of the room, but his church sent me $250 to spend while I was there! Many thanks to the Rochester Worldwide Church of God congregation! I had the greatest time ever while I was there, and I sure did appreciate the break from work. I had asked for prayers earlier for my pumpkin crop and finances, so quite a few people asked about my situation. One lady, Muriel, wanted to buy a "none pumpkin". So she gave me $20 for a "none pumpkin"!

Doug Johannsen planned a surprise retirement dinner for David Fiedler, as he will be retiring this December from his job as our regional pastor. I knew of this meal sometime beforehand and decided that I wouldn't go because I figured there would be many there far more important than I. The night before, though, Doug invited me to be there and said that he would buy my meal. So I figured, "Who can resist a deal like that?" I felt very privileged to be around that table. We all got to roast David. I told about the time at the Illinois camp when we were going to catch the hornets. Several of us were ready to do what we had to do to eliminate them. We were waiting for Dave to show up and we finally found him at the camp store buying ice cream! As the evening went on, I told David, Linda Holms and Cherry and Tracy Porter some funny stories from days gone by, when all my nephews were little. Linda thought I should write about them sometime, so here they are.

One time, fifteen to twenty years ago when my nephews Nate, Zack, Mitch, Adam, Dustin and Matt were little, they were in the garden that my mother used to keep. I had just finished with the cattle chores before supper. As I came up from the barn, I noticed those guys all out in the garden throwing carrot tops into the air, having a high old time! I asked them what in the world they were doing in Grandma's garden? Their response was, "We're being Bugs Bunny!" "Well, I'm Elmer Fudd," I said, "and if you don't get out of there, you are going to get it!" They all tore out of there like instantly! The memory of that still makes me laugh!

Another time my sister, Jane, was watching her boys playing out by the car. A short time later, Matt walked into the house telling her that Dustin was locked in the trunk of the car, but she didn't need to worry, because Dustin had the keys with him! Jane had to call 911 and the rescue squad came out to get Dustin out of the trunk. I guess he was a comical sight when the trunk door was opened and he was able to climb out.

I had noticed Willard High get up from the dinner table and walk away. So I told Tracy and Cherry about the time Willard was giving a session on listening to God, some place a few years back. Willard had used the scripture,

Job 33:14-15: For God does speak - now one way, now another - though man may not perceive it. In a dream, in a vision of the night, when deep sleep falls on men as they slumber in their beds...

As usual, I was starting to fall asleep while Willard was trying to make his point, Willard said "Now, don't go to sleep on me!" I knew he had me in mind when he said this. I just laughed to myself and thought, "Well, Willard, how am I supposed to hear from God if I can't get to sleep?" My listeners got a chuckle out of that one!

I think I also told them about the time my banker fell into the mud hole, but I will save that one for some other time!

I will miss David. He made a statement at camp one time that has forever changed the way I look at our youth. The first year we had camp at Illinois, we had some pretty tough personalities there! Everyone was about at the end of their ropes dealing with them. I remember asking one pastor how his week was going when I saw him on a walk. He said he would just like to choke everybody! That evening David called all staff for a meeting down at the chapel. He said, "You know these youth have to see Jesus in us. But something just as important, we have to see Jesus in them." And you know what? You *could* see Jesus in them, even though in a few, he was a little harder see! I told this to David at the close of the Dells celebration, and that also pointed out that some of those youth where Jesus was a little harder to see, were there this weekend. One of them even signed up to be a counselor for next year's camp! What an incredible miracle!

As the celebration came to a close, I told my friend, Tracy Porter, that it was sure hard to leave all of this! I don't think there were too many dry eyes in the place! As I was saying goodbye to some people I knew, my friend, Kevin from camp, shoved something in my pocket and said "Make sure you have a steak on me!" (Which I did, Kevin!) Tracy also shoved something in my pocket and told me to let him know how everything worked out for me this fall! (So, Tracy, when you get done reading this story, you will know how things have worked out!) On my way home, I remembered what was shoved into my pocket. I went to the Dells with $325 in my pocket. I really didn't spend much while I was there, so I thought I would give a $100 offering. But I was coming home with $600! I prayed a blessing on those that gave this and remembered a time that I was able to give generously to a young man I knew in seminary. He had asked if it would be possible if somebody could send him some money for stamps. I had just made a big sale of hay, so I sent him a check for $500. He told me that he had almost tipped over when he opened the letter and that I had no idea how much that had helped him out!

Matt.10:8: *Freely you have received, freely give.*

I have been in both situations now - able to give and able to receive. It seems it takes a little getting used to when you're the one that has to do the receiving, and it is far better to be in a position to be able to give!

Before I went to the Dells, I had asked God for provision to publish my next book. Since I feel that the people who gave me these funds were being prompted by the Holy Spirit, that's where they will be used. From the messages that I heard while I was there, I had to admit that I didn't know Jesus quite as well as I thought I did. So my prayers since then have been that this triune God of ours – Father, Son, and Holy Spirit - show me the way that he wants me to know him instead of the way that I think that I know him! Since I've been praying this way, some interesting things have been taking place. I have felt for some time now that God isn't always who you think he is!

The day after I returned home from the Dells, I was tending to some things down at my pumpkin stand. A woman named Margo stopped by. I learned that Margo attended the "Jesus church" in St. Peter, MN. Margo told me that she felt that God had sent her out here today because she had felt so depressed that morning, she didn't want to even get out of bed. She went on to say that she had read a few of my stories from my book and that they had really encouraged her! I told Margo that her saying that encouraged me. She said she didn't know what God was up to in her life, because her husband had cancer and doctors had told her that her granddaughter would never be able to walk again. I shared with her three stories of mine where God had healed me, and said that I would pray for her husband and granddaughter. After our conversation, I went back to work stocking the stand. Margo continued to shop for pumpkins, but before she left she walked up to me and told me that God had told her to give me this. She said she'd learned over the years to be obedient to his voice, and handed me a $100 bill! All I could say was, "God bless you, Margo!" And now I had $700 for my book!

The very next morning I was on my way to town to pay a bill. I actually had a second bill to pay, but I needed another $50. I stopped down at the pumpkin stand on my way to town. I wanted to check the money box, just in case there might be enough in there to pay the other bill. I unlocked the lid, but all that was inside was a $5 dollar bill. Since I needed $50 dollars to pay the other bill, I decided $5 wasn't enough to mess around with. So I let it fall to the bottom of the box and shut the lid on old Abe and locked it. About an hour later, I was loading some corn bundles for the stand and I noticed a white car pull in there. By the time I drove down with my load, the white car had gone. I decided to check the money box just to see what was in it now. I unlocked the lid. There was a $20 dollar bill and a $50 dollar bill in there, but no $5 bill. It had completely vanished! It is completely impossible for anyone to get into that box without a key. And I do believe I can tell the difference between a $5 bill and a $50 dollar bill, especially when I could've used the $50 not more than an hour earlier! I now had $750 for my book!

Sometime that same week, Pete Wolf, a neighbor of mine, wanted me to help him move some round bales and he also wanted to buy a load of hay. I charged Pete $200 to load and unload the hay. I now had $950 for my book! That Sunday, one week after I came home from the Dells, Doug Johannsen arranged to have a potluck meal at my farm. We normally have a fundraiser here in the fall for our winter camp, Snowblast. However, this year with the poor pumpkin crop, it was just not possible. Doug thought we should have a potluck meal, anyway. So with me not being the best of housekeepers, I hired Christine Trickey to clean my house. I thought it was a miracle that when Christine saw my house, she didn't take off running! I guess housekeeping isn't top priority for me. After all, doesn't it say in Proverbs 24:27 *"Finish your outdoor work and get your field ready; after that build your house"?*

When Christine was finished, I asked her what I owed her? She had came around noon and worked till past 7:00 p.m.! She thought for a while and said, "Well, we are supposed to share one another's burdens." I know she was thinking about Galatians 6:2 *Carry each others' burdens, and in this way you will fulfill the law of Christ.*

"How about $100?" she said after some thought. "But you have to promise me to get rid of the old pillows that you have and get some new ones and don't wait so long to call me next time!" So I promised. Sunday came and we had plenty of food and conversation. A couple of people brought cards, so I put them aside to open later. Doug told me that Carolyn Lane was interested in editing my book, something she would do for free because of the year I'd had. That saves me from hiring someone to do it. What an incredible blessing! After everyone had left, I remembered the cards. Between the two cards, there were $1100 dollars in them! Wow! In just ten days God had answered my prayers for provision for my book to be published, using about ten people. None had knowledge of how I was going to use their gift, for except for Carolyn! God never ceases to amaze me!

Late last winter I had it in my mind that I needed to have some new signs made. I wanted to use the cover of my book for my new signs, because I felt that was something God had given me. I also wanted to add my phone number someplace on the sign. I would use a four by eight sheet of plywood, so it would look just like my book cover. These would replace my old hay signs, because my life was not about just selling hay any more. Pastor Todd Fox once preached a sermon about having maximum impact for Jesus Christ in our area of influence. For me, that would be these signs - kind of like when God changed Abram's name to Abraham.

> **Genesis 17:5** *No longer will you be called Abram: your name will be Abraham, for I have made you a father of many nations.*

So from now on, instead of "Hay By George!" My signs would read "Hey By George!" for I am trying to give God the glory through my stories and not just trying to sell hay. I have no Idea what implications this will have for me. I doubt it will have the same magnitude that it had for Abraham. Maybe it means I will starve, but so far there is subtle difference! Everyone still calls me about hay. I had pretty much given up the idea for these signs because of the year I had and the cost involved. Plus, I really didn't know anyone personally to help me with this Idea, so that generally causes me to procrastinate even more.

Then, on the 22nd of October, I noticed a missed call on my cell phone. I dialed the number and the guy on the other end answered "Sign Pro". I told the guy that this number was on my cell phone and I was just returning the call. He said he didn't know who could've called me, but it wasn't him and he was the only one still there because the time was 5:30 p.m. Hmm, strange! Later that evening, I received a call from a person who wanted some firewood. I wasn't 100 percent sure, because he was talking kind of fast, but I thought he said his name was Steve Denn. When I delivered the wood on Friday, I saw a sign on the side of his house. It said "Welcome to the Denn's." I asked Steve if we were related because we had the same last name. Steve told me that he didn't know, because he had just moved to Mankato on the 15th of April from Nebraska. The only other Denns he knew were his dad and grandfather. I told Steve that I would be surprised if we were not related, because it's not a very common last name, and I haven't met a Denn yet who I wasn't related to somehow! I asked Steve what he did for a living. He told me he was the sales manager for Sign Pro, a place that makes signs in lower North Mankato. Until that time, I had practically given up hope for these new signs to become a reality! I told Steve my idea and asked if they could do it. "Yeah, it would be easy" he said. It would be a little expensive, but the more I had made, the cheaper it would be.

The next Monday, I was at the bank after wondering about this sign thing all weekend. I asked God to give me a sign if this was all from him, because this would be kind of expensive and I had other bills I should pay. Well, there was only one way to find out. I called Steve to see if he was in, and he was. I asked if we could get together about this sign Idea of mine, and if he was available, I would be right down there. After we met, I told him I would need three signs – one that was four feet by eight feet on both sides, and two with the same dimensions, one sided. Last spring, I had purchased the cover of my book on CD because I figured I would need it if I found someone to do the signs. Steve punched all the information I had given him into his computer, then turned his screen so I could see it. The total cost would be $2222.06 cost. I knew immediately that this was from God! The idea for the book cover came about from a men's fishing retreat two winters ago on the second week in February. It consisted of 222 KBs when I sent it in for publishing and I started that process on the 22nd of February. Last winter my dad, whose name is Albert, went to alcohol treatment in Albert Lee, MN. I gave a copy of my book to a lady named Grace (my Dad's couch/counselor) for her birthday, which was on February 22! Also, there were two other instances when I saw this sequence of numbers that turned out to have God's hand in them, but I won't go into them now.

Steve told me that this was really unusual because they could have the signs finished this week because I had everything that we needed for the graphics. Well, the whole thing seemed rather inexplicable! They were done on Thursday, I picked them up on Friday, and Terry and I put them up on Saturday. The last two signs went up on a 22 acre field that I farm by Elysian, MN. On our way over to put them up, a car passed us with license plate number 222. I just laughed when I saw it! It really makes me wonder what God is up to!

After that, all that was left to do was get the plowing done. It took about a week to do that. It has been always interesting to watch the sea gulls follow the plow looking for worms to eat. They will stay with you all day, and then when evening comes, suddenly they are gone! Often they fly so close you can see their beady little eyes and often I wondered what in the world this white bird was good for. Just tonight I heard a story about some guys during WWII that were stranded on the ocean for a month without food or water. One day a sea gull landed on one of their heads. They were able to eat the sea gull and use its entrails for fishing string. Because of that, they were able to stay alive until they were rescued. I guess after hearing that story, I will never look at them as a useless bird again! Well, the plowing is done and the threshing is done and so brings the close to another season, but then I have rambled on here!

It's now the 15th of November and that means that my rent is due today for my farmland. "What," I ask myself, "am I going to do?" I keep praying and asking God for a miracle! After a few phone calls to people that owe me some money, I find that by Wednesday I can come up with half the rent. I was busy until 3:30 p.m., so now I have to make the call that could change my life! What will my landlord say? First, I say a prayer for the right words to say and that the Holy Spirit would be present during our phone conversation, because remember, this is the first time in 47 years that I was late with the rent! I made the call immediately after I prayed. "Bob," I said, "I hate to tell you this, but I can't come up with all the rent just yet. I can give you $2000 today and another $2000 on Wednesday and after that, I can't pay you until some hay sells, whenever that may be!" "That's OK." Bob said "You just pay me when you can."

So there you are!

This evening as I drove up to see my Father, I saw this license plate as a car went past – "He is 4U!"

Genesis 8:22: As long as the earth endures, seed time and harvest, cold and heat, summer and winter, day and night will never cease.

I reckon that God's purpose for me in all of this seems to be right here - on the Northwest side of Wita Lake!

God's peace and abundant blessings to you all!

Your brother in Christ,

George Denn

Epilogue

As I look back over the past three years here on the farm, I realize that a lot of the work that went on here, the people I have met, and even several of the stories you just read came about because of a huge wind storm that came through here three years ago. It wrecked the two barns that used to be here and uprooted countless old trees! The storm left the place looking terrible! I remember the next evening before I went to sleep; I was listening to a story on the radio. In the story, a man had been walking on the beach of the ocean after a storm. As he walked, he came across some old coins that had been washed up on shore by the storm. They were very valuable coins. He learned that they were part of a ship's cargo that had sunk from a storm some 300 years earlier! The moral of the story was that we should look for the treasure out of the storm. I thought "How on earth can I find treasure in all of this?"

Now some three years later, I have found the treasure in that storm. My friend, Doug Johannsen, has made quite a few picture frames from the old barn's wood. They hang in several homes, and one is at Eagle Bluff Environmental Center in southeastern Minnesota! My friend, Jeff Peterson, made a tree house for his kids out of the lumber from the second barn that I'd built in 1988. Ethan Gibson helped me saw up all the downed trees, as well as helped split and stack it, along with Joseph Kruse, Brad Claggett and Terry Trickey. It has given me winter income for the past two years from firewood sales! But the real treasure that I found was not in the money for the firewood! It was found in the friendships that were forged because of the storm! When I see the picture frames from the old barn, or see the tree house, or visit with one of the friends that I have come to know because of the storm, I realize that it's within these things that I have found the treasure out of the storm!

Forty-seven years ago, the first day that my Dad and Mom arrived here, a man who was moving his cows off our farm laughed at my Dad and asked him, "What do you want this frog farm for?" He said this because it was pretty common knowledge that this farm is wet and not well drained. Also, possibly because my Dad was fairly young, yet just thirty years of age, and didn't know what he was getting himself into. In the past fifteen years of my life here, I have come to see the treasure in that man's words! I use the word "frog" as an acronym, which to me means, "Fully Rely On God". And it is within that word that I have found the true wealth of this farm!

—George W. Denn

If the Holy Spirit leads you to comment, please send a note to:
George Denn
59381 243rd St.
Kasota Minnesota 56050

About the Author

George W. Denn is a fifth generation farmer from southern Minnesota. Now at age 47, he has actively been engaged in full time farming since age sixteen. The land he operates lies within Blue Earth, Le Sueur, and Waseca counties. He is a member of the Worldwide Church of God, is active in youth ministry, and is now the author of two books, <u>Hey By George!</u> and <u>On the Northwest Side of Wita Lake</u>. Although once recognized for his "<u>Hay By George!</u>" slogans that were common in southern Minnesota, George was challenged by a sermon he once heard about "having maximum impact for Jesus Christ in his area of influence". He tore down the old hay signs and made the new signs that are in existence today! Instead of selling hay, the signs now serve to glorify God and what he has done in George's life by promoting the books and stories he has written. George resides on the same farm that he writes about in rural Minnesota.

CPSIA information can be obtained at www.ICGtesting.com
Printed in the USA
BVOW04s2316220916

463049BV00001B/2/P